SCDA

Beyond Boundaries

ORO EDITIONS

SCDA

www.scdaarchitects.com
SINGAPORE / SHANGHAI / NEW YORK

Foreword

Soo K Chan

"Space" is an immeasurable and unfixed term. Its meaning is impossible to define in a singular manner, yet everyone has a perception of its value. Space is a physical parameter; it captures a volumetric reading. It is, however, also a conceptual notion. In this way, we can see architecture in particular, as both enclosing space and giving an *idea* of space. Previously a word common only within philosophical discourse, in architecture, the term was introduced as part of the development of modernism and its terminology still dominates our lexicon.[1]

In fact, notions of space are the basis of nearly all theories that have shaped the architectural movements of the past century—whether as reactions against or extensions of the spatial propositions of modernism. Space will continue to be a shifting concept that, precisely in its undefined nature, offers much opportunity for exploration and experimentation.

In the following pages, we're as interested in space as in the relationships between spaces. To encapsulate as broad an understanding of space as possible, we rely both on more classically rooted terminology that evokes ideas of space, such as procession, order, enclosure, transitions, and more contemporary terms like "spatial plasticity," a consideration of the relationship of spaces to each other and to the whole.

A space for living is the most fundamental need of people and, by extension, how we live together within units, within buildings, within cities, and within the world must be very carefully considered. Many notable architects in modern history have reimagined the future of residential space. Le Corbusier saw the house as a machine for living, Mies van der Rohe brought in light through precision and assemblage via the development of the curtainwall, and Frank Lloyd Wright strove for an integration of organic architecture and nature. We can learn from each of these precedents—some strategies work and some do not.

Over the years, as SCDA's projects grew in scope and complexity, we have had similar opportunities to rethink high density housing, with projects in different locations with different climates, and with different budgets to test these ideas. It has urged us to examine the role landscape plays in our designs, as the programmatic components of housing becomes repetitive and subject to rigid local building codes. The landscape components can organize and define the spatial principle within our design vocabulary.

With projects all over the world, we know that one singular strategy will never make for a successful solution. However, our basic needs are universal. We can rely on the fact that the quality of our spatial environments impacts our health—light and air are required for our wellbeing—and we cannot live in artificial silos; we need to be connected to nature in some way.

In this monograph, we have gathered projects, spanning over 12 years, to explore how we design and put buildings together. Assessing one's own work is often a worthy and illuminating exercise. In past publications, we have felt the luxury of receiving outside perspectives. Aaron Betsky has characterized SCDA's practice as one suspended between emerging technology and different cultures, while Leon van Schaik has argued for a distancing from these dual realities.[2] He instead suggests a utopian search for perfection: in each work, no matter the context, practice makes perfect. It is not implausible that the two characterizations early 1990s, to his roots in Asia, convinced that architecture is underpinned by a syntax, a set of rules, safety rails... amongst which he mentions figure-ground. Did he encounter Colin Rowe, the guru of this method, I wonder? Certainly, his designs, even in the early years of his practice, display an intensely worked craftsmanship in the alternating of spaces and solids. He talks of becoming intensely aware of the hierarchies of circulation in eastern palaces, the Forbidden City, for example. And you can see what he means when you look at the planning of the resorts. In the resorts too, his respect for the ephemerality of Japanese traditional architecture is observable.

The besetting sin of modernist education lay in the idea of "originality." Soo Khian's 1980s mentors aimed to correct that by going into history. I have become interested in two models for relating to the history of a discipline, now that we all accept that we cannot slough off our histories. One, adopted by the post-modernists, is to internalize the past as an ideal model and attempt to replicate it in new conditions. The other is to treat the past as a commons across which trails can be ventured. You might expect me to place Soo Khian in the first camp, since I have previously identified him as an idealist. But I do not. To me, it is the pathway that Soo Khian has steadfastly developed and persevered, and with that puts him in the second category—that of those who seek out the processes, the underlying syntaxes, and work with those rather than with their entirely contingent manifestations in other peoples' work.

Soo Khian was—maybe is still—a creature of the globalized world: happy at a moment's notice to leap onto a flight to New York.

Yet he talks of the way in which the pandemic that began in 2019 has been used in cities around the world to create huge improvements to how we live in cities. Pavements have been enlarged into social spaces, alternative modes of transport have been encouraged, and social distancing has civilized airports—places that had become frenetically horrid. Small steps, but achievable and with measurable impacts on our general well-being. Maybe this slow change to our urban pathways (which can be well or badly implemented) informs his view, which I strongly agree with, that architects—while they can help others where there is a political will—cannot, by themselves, save the world.

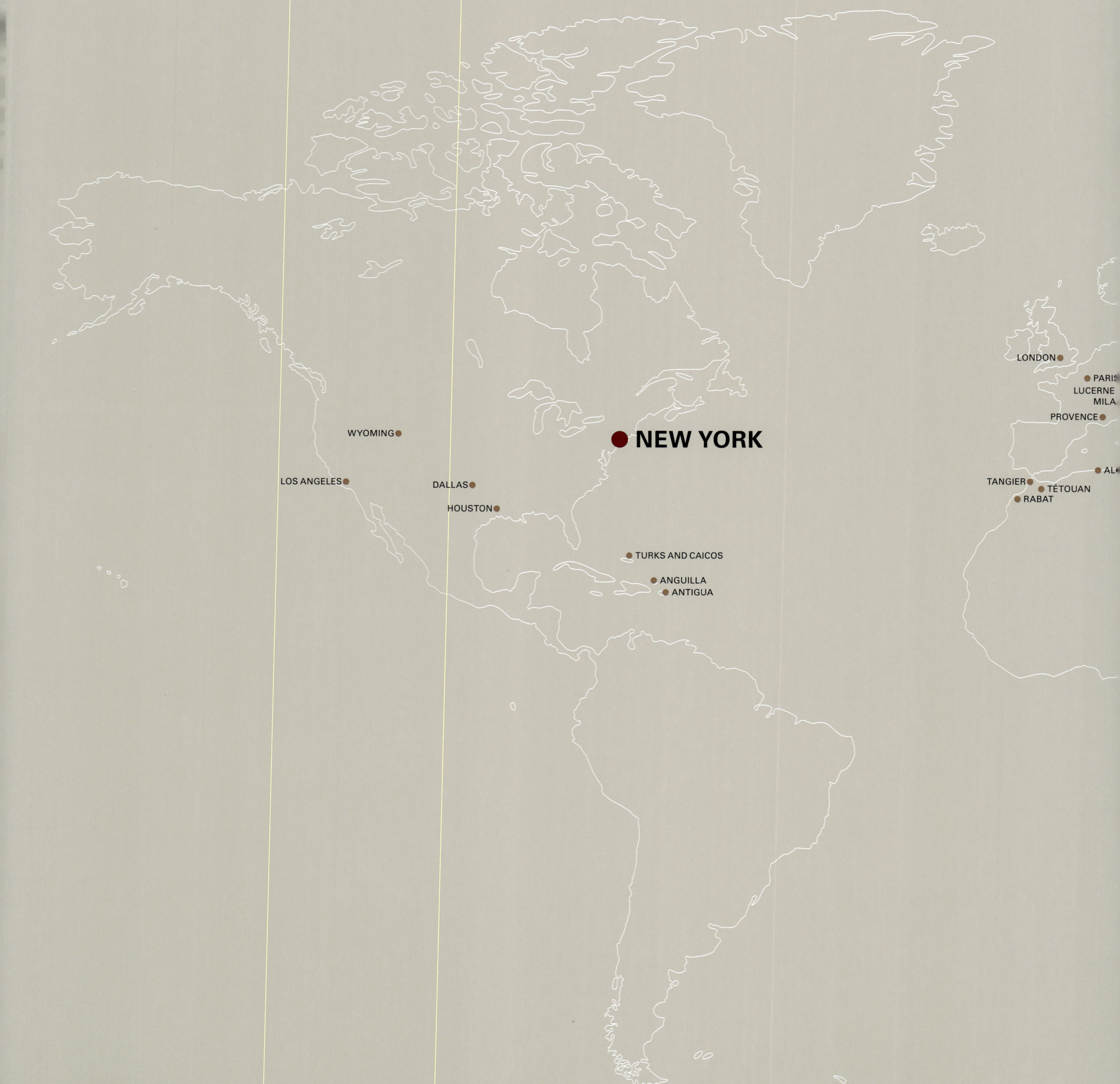
NEW YORK
WYOMING
LOS ANGELES
DALLAS
HOUSTON
TURKS AND CAICOS
ANGUILLA
ANTIGUA
LONDON
PARIS
LUCERNE
MILA
PROVENCE
AL
TANGIER
TÉTOUAN
RABAT

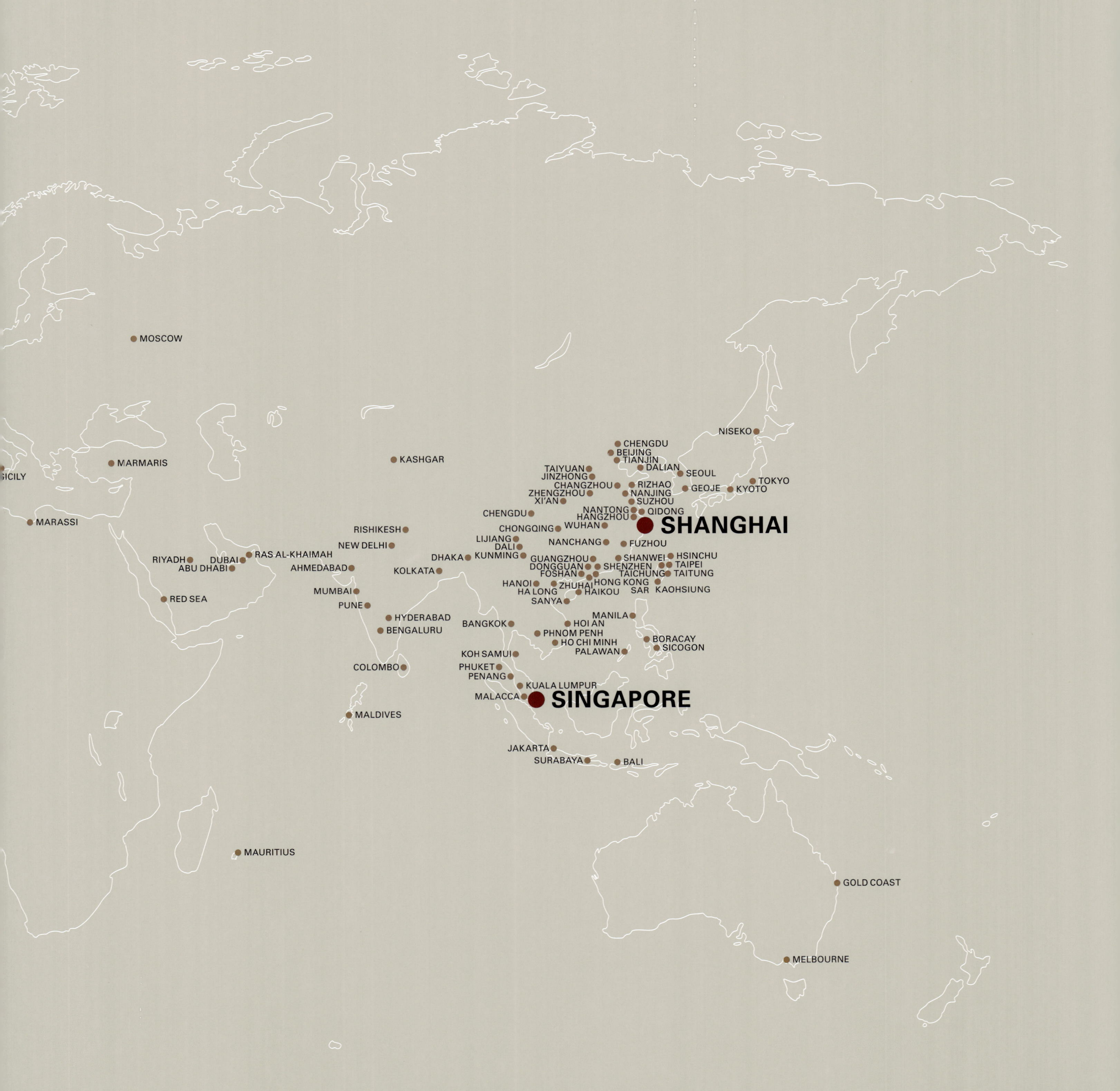

PROJECT LOCATIONS: WORLDWIDE

High Density and Mixed-use

La Cadiere Garden City
Poly Shanghai
Soori High Line
Park Lane
515 High Line Residences
Azabudai Hills Residential
Banyan Tree Residences
Capri Bukit Bintang
Savyavasa
19 Nassim
SkyTerrace@Dawson
OCT Tian E Bao
The Sanya Edition
La Cadiere Lakeside City
Amber Park
Rivière
IHG Robertson Quay
The Lalu
Vanke Hangzhou
Jumeirah Residences
Mattel Shenzhen
Vanke Daxiang
OUE Downtown
Seventy
Juhu Beach Residence
Alibaug Lodha
Cuscaden Reserve
Cluny Park Residence
Seletar Park Residences

LA CADIERE GARDEN CITY

Chengdu, China, 2017

In today's globalized world, cities often lack distinctiveness and green communal spaces, leading to a need for environments that evoke emotions and create lasting impressions.

SCDA's design draws inspiration from an era of monumental architecture, seeking to juxtapose towering structures with serene natural surroundings. The vision is to integrate expansive green spaces into the fabric of the development, creating a contrast between the solidity of the buildings and the ethereal beauty of the landscape.

The massing and composition of the towers are defined to establish a commanding architectural presence within the master plan. This collection of towers, designed and built over several phases serve as a backdrop to the skyline of the garden city. Green spaces are envisioned as dynamic, folded planes that emerge from the ground, dividing the area into various sheltered, landscaped plazas.

The urban strategy focuses on creating connectivity between the site and the lake, with the towers positioned along a folded landscape spine to integrate with the lakeside and parkland. This composition provides a striking vista for pedestrians and defines inviting plazas for events and gatherings. The undulating landscape and shaded walkways offer tranquil spaces for relaxation, while a private clubhouse nestled within the landscape provides amenities for residents.

The towers, clad in glazed ceramic fins, convey a sense of verticality and aspiration, symbolizing a harmonious coexistence with nature while offering uninterrupted views of the parkland, lake, and distant mountains.

La Cadiere Garden City stands as a landmark addition to Chengdu's new city center, surrounded by a sprawling central park, picturesque lake, and abundant natural pathways.

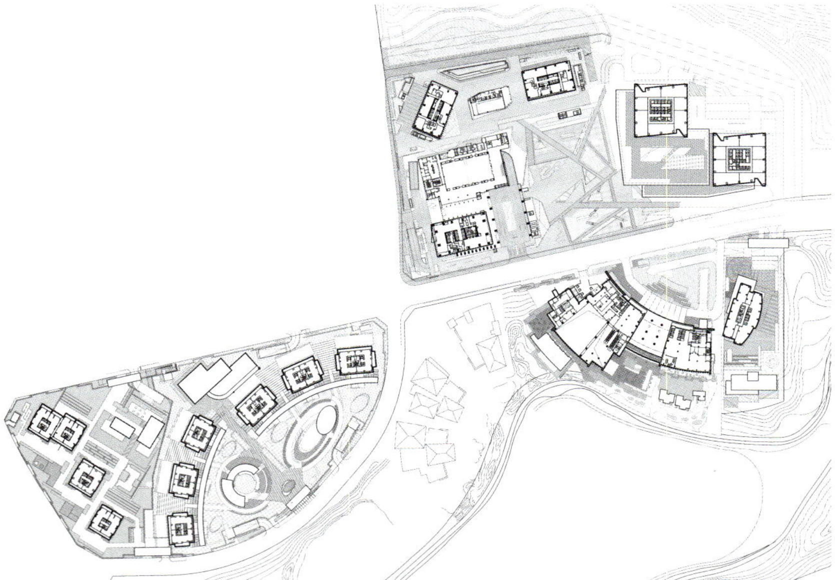

LA CADIERE GARDEN CITY

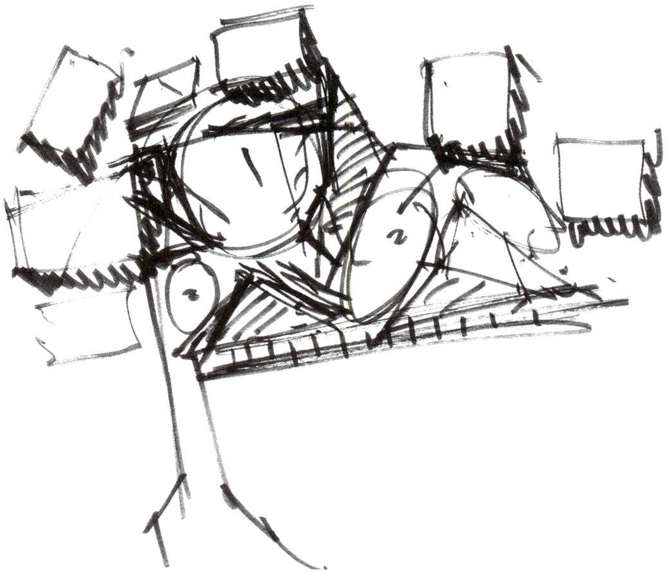

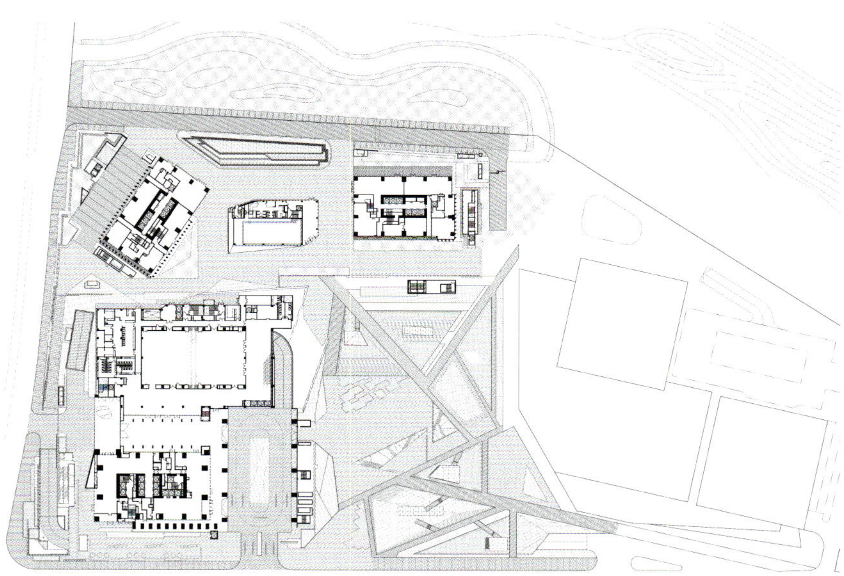

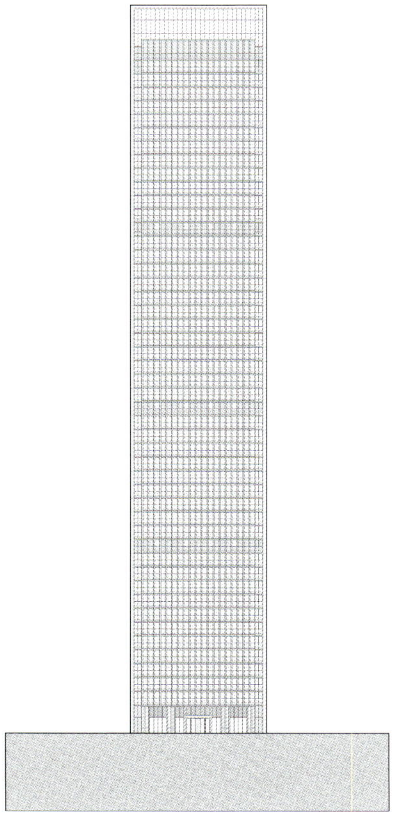

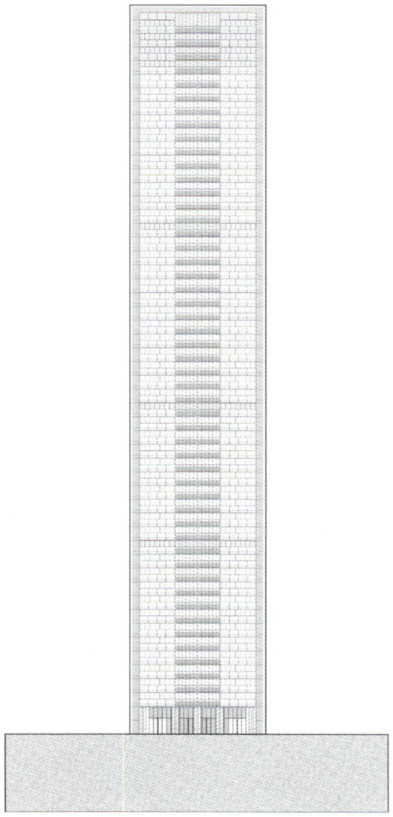

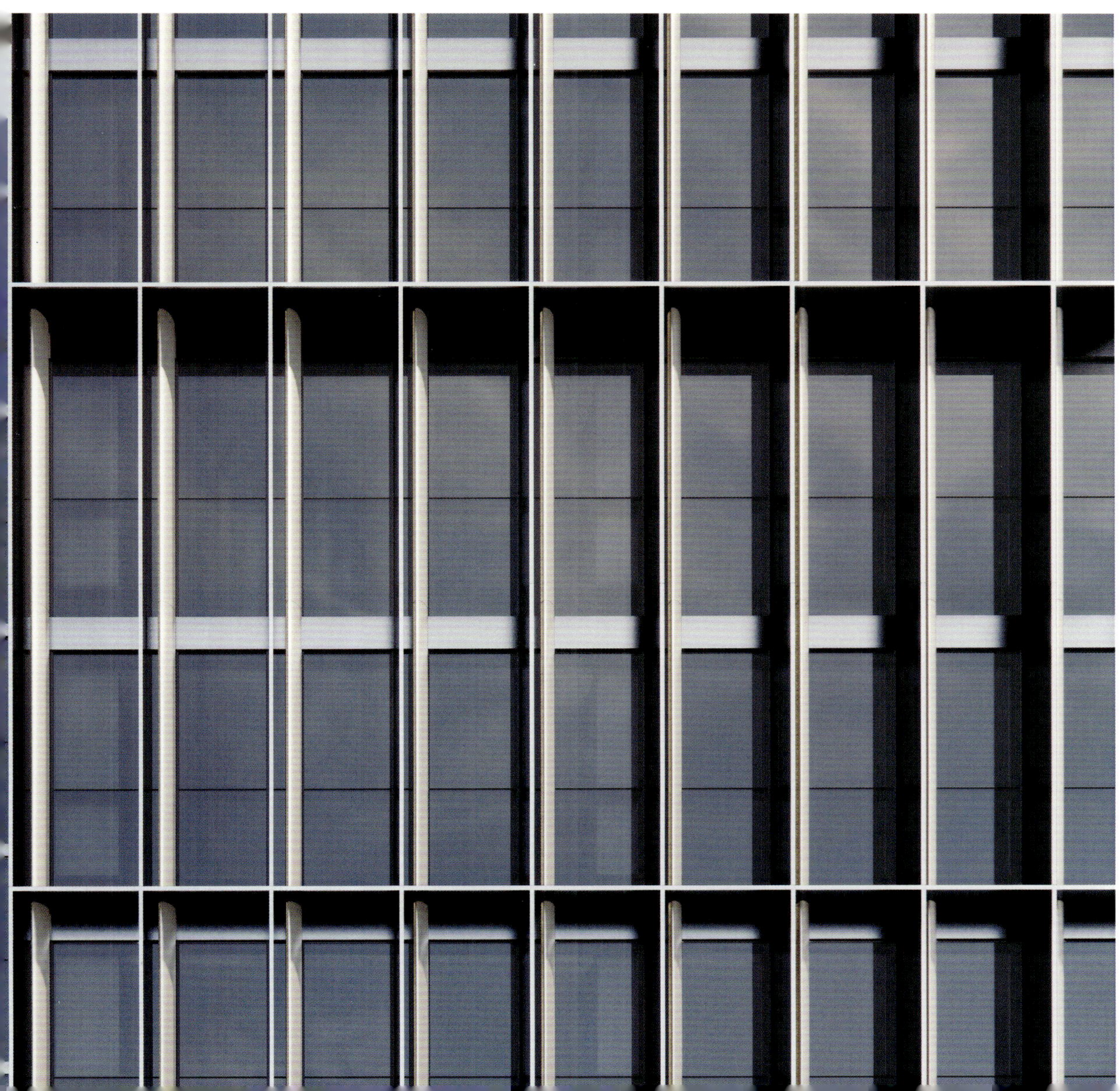

POLY SHANGHAI

Shanghai, China, 2018

Located between the Pudong and Puxi urban cores, the project site commands attention, offering a prime opportunity to reshape the Shanghai skyline. The site's historic legacy as the residential component of the 2010 World Expo serves as a foundation of inspiration for the design of the master plan and architectural expression of the residential towers. The design aims to create a timeless modernist architecture, providing a serene living environment and unparalleled city and river views.

Throughout the design process, implementation of clear spatial hierarchies and structural order were given priority. These metaphysical prioritizations stitch spaces together through a cohesive understanding of light and form.

Structural order, guided by an acute application of an articulated architectural language, elevates a sense of monumentality to the towers while maintaining a clarity of refined scale and proportion of the individual elements. The architectural façade design incorporates interlocking vertical and horizontal elements responding to the texture of existing expo buildings. The façade elements are extensions of the interior spaces, with metal profiles reflecting the precision and intricacy of a contemporary architectural language. Double-height balconies, as extensions of indoor dining areas, blur the boundaries between indoor and outdoor spaces, seamlessly bringing the Huangpu River views into the interior.

The development's attention to public space ensures a holistic experience from exterior to interior. The journey from the drop-off pavilion to the reception lobby, clubhouse, and sunken courtyard is enlivened by continuous covered galleries, formal lawns, lush greenery and water features that integrate into the overall landscape environment.

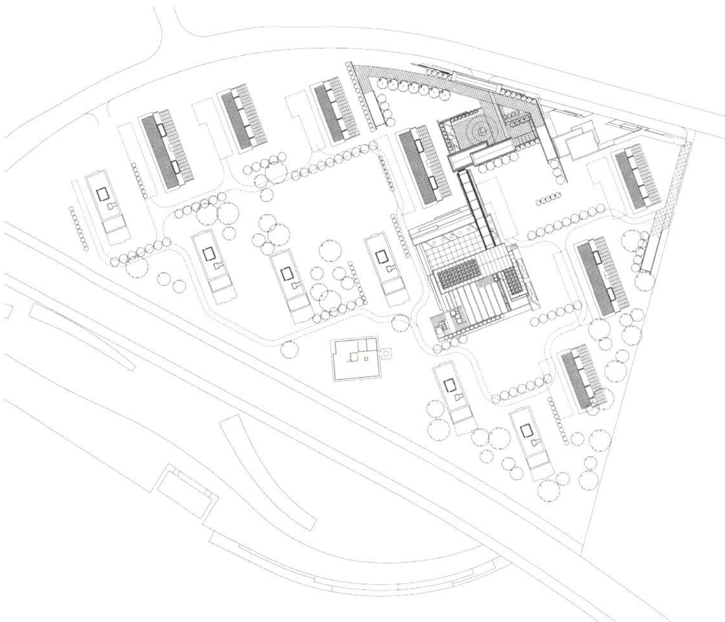

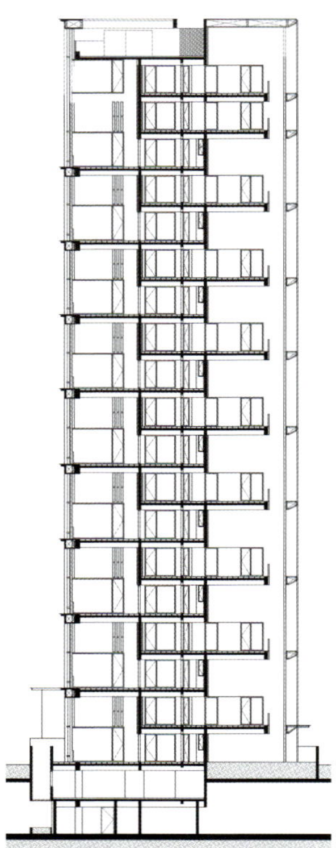

POLY SHANGHAI

SOORI HIGH LINE

New York, USA, 2012

Soori High Line, a boutique residential development in West Chelsea, Lower Manhattan, is located adjacent to the renowned High Line Park: a 1.45-mile urban park converted from a former elevated freight rail road. Facing West 29th Street, the 11-story building comprises a mix of one- to five-bedroom luxury apartments, featuring private recreational amenities and a well-appointed ground-floor lobby.

Approaching the Soori, guests are welcomed by a series of monolithic wood louvers towering above the busy street below.

This subtlety of modernity and warmth stands in stark contrast to the building's harsh surroundings of glass and steel. These fins form a staggered veil in front of large glass façade panels, providing privacy for residents and character to the local urban fabric. Double-volume living and dining spaces are situated at the building's forefront and extend internally to private pools recessed within the structure. Each private pool runs from the master suite along the living areas, offering views outward. Transparent pool edges enhance visual connectivity and serve as integral façade elements.

The unit layout maximizes spatial hierarchy, with high ceilings and ample living space. Units are organized to include either duplex configurations or smaller units facing rear gardens, culminating in a four-level penthouse with its own private terrace and rooftop pool overlooking Hudson Yards.

Soori High Line exhibits a refined palette of elements, a combination of horizontality and verticality, full-height glass, warm accents, and ambient lighting. The architecture and interiors are displayed as a visual showcase from the street, harmonizing with Manhattan's historical urban backdrop. The interplay of materials and spatial arrangement contributes to a timeless architectural addition to the street, reflecting the ongoing revitalization of the High Line and its surroundings.

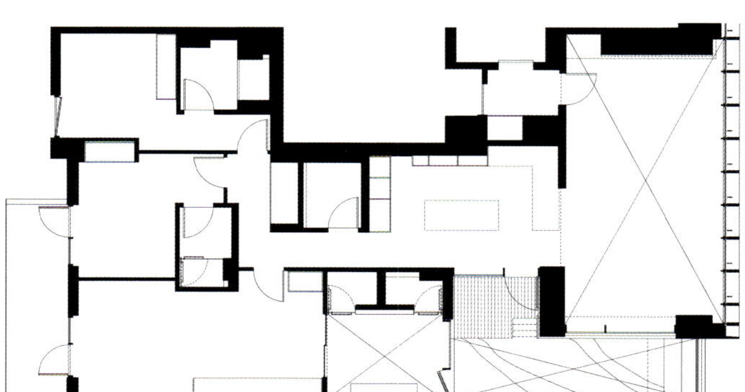

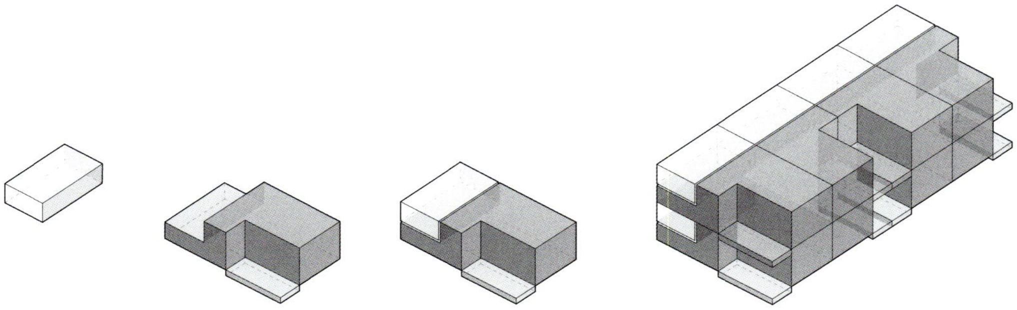

GENERAC
INDUSTRIAL
POWER

PARK LANE

New York, USA, 2022

The Park Lane development is sited in one of the most visible sites in New York City, overlooking the length of Central Park and shoulder-to-shoulder with some of the tallest residential projects in the city. Conceptualized as a large residential "sky apartment" rising to over 400-feet, the building would replace the existing Park Lane hotel and occupy the gap site created by its removal. The location directly fronting Central Park became its inspiration to embody volume and greenery within its high-rise residential typology.

The tower is composed by interlocking four- and five-bedroom modules of simplex units creating two-story sky gardens for each unit. The sky gardens can be enclosed in winter, creating semi-conditioned space, an extension of the living/dining areas.

The building expresses the modularity of the interlocking units, expressing them truthfully on the façade as the tower rises to break down the conventional monotony of a curtain wall skin. The play of internal and external volume within each module allows for the introduction of green space in each stack, creating a dialogue between the tower and the greenery of Central Park.

To further accentuate the modularity, the building adopts glass of different tones and reflectivity, segmenting the tower into larger 12-story modules framed by deep architectural "ribbons" winding down the tower façade. The composition and expression of the tower's program would create a district identity for the building, differentiating it from the conventional and prevalent glass skin towers.

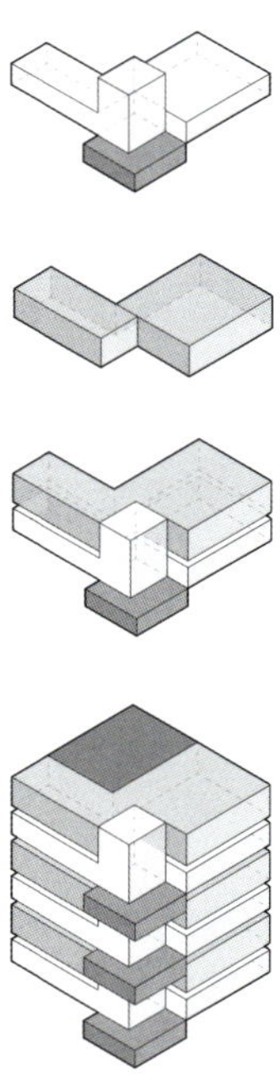

515 HIGH LINE RESIDENCES

New York, USA, 2016

515 West 29th Street in the West Chelsea district of New York occupies a highly visible corner site fronting both the High Line elevated landscape park and the busy commercial plaza of Hudson Yards. The location necessitated a sculptural approach to the treatment of the building, where the building is broken down into three stacked, shifting volumes, transitioning between the urban scale of a city skyscraper, to the pedestrian scale of the sidewalk.

A glass box sits perched above the existing base envelope of the original building. A sensitive insertion of structure and program created a series of two- and three-bedroom apartments, stacked with deep terraces and double-height volumes for the larger units. The units were arranged around a side core to ensure views on all three aspects of the building were prioritized.

The façade, composed of rows of overlapping vertical curved glass fins create an undulating, dynamic surface recalling the movement of the city and serving as an architectural register to the changing seasons, much like the shifting, lush landscapes of the High Line. At its peak, the building culminates in a sharp, up-lit, mesh-clad crown, floating above generous outdoor terraces, the perfect vantage points from which to observe the city below.

The interior of the 515 juxtaposes modern living with the neighborhood's profoundly urban and industrial roots. Concrete panels in the lobby serve as an urbane transition into well-appointed residences, where a minimal aesthetic combines with a textured material palette, taking one from warm, textured woods to smooth, calm stone.

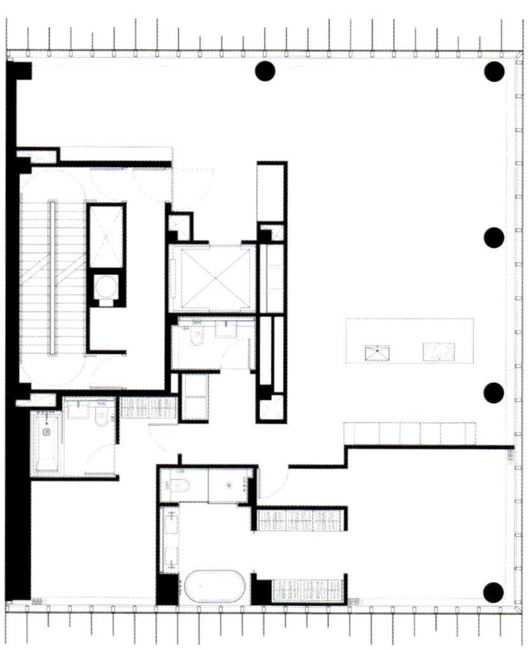

AZABUDAI HILLS RESIDENTIAL

Tokyo, Japan, 2016

Centrally located within the heart of Tokyo, the Azabudai master plan was conceived as a vibrant new district, providing residential, commercial, retail, and institutional spaces within the city. At the heart of the development is a large central park with connected green public space accessible to the adjacent towers, a distinct new environment on a large urban scale.

The concept for the residential tower was to create a series of footprints accommodating a variety of unit types, with a strong relationship to the proposed central green park.

The massing concept explored the integration of deep and high volumetric "cuts" into the building bringing natural light and ventilation to the units and common circulation areas. The large floor plate and resultant building mass was broken down by the subtraction of volume, spaces that would be activated by greenery and connected to each corner unit. Each cut out consists of a 12-story volume sectionally divided into six double-volume private terraces connected to living/dining and entertainment areas. The 12-story cut-outs alternate in each of the four sections of building modules as the building rises, visually breaking down the impact of the tower's mass.

Each apartment was conceived as interlocking modules of four- and five-bedroom units, with generous two-story spaces afforded to both its interior and exterior space. The larger units, located in the upper modules of the building are accessed by direct private lift. These units are integrated with private pools and expansive terraces, located at the corner of each wing to maximize the views over central Tokyo.

AZABUDAI HILLS RESIDENTIAL

BAAN CHAOPRAYA

BANYAN TREE RESIDENCES

Bangkok, Thailand, 2016

The Banyan Tree Riverside Residences stands as a singular architectural statement on the banks of the Chao Phraya. The design ethos gravitates towards formal simplicity enriched with crafted detailing. The all-glass façade, both transparent and ephemeral, reflects and embodies the movement of the river below.

The 45-story condominium presents maximum frontage towards the Chao Phraya, ensuring all units enjoy unobstructed views of the surrounding natural and urban landscapes. Upon entry, the main tower and podium displays a sculptural perforated screen, multifaceted and geometric, giving the tower its distinct identity on the riverfront skyline. In the evening, lighting further illuminates and accentuates the singularity of this undulating sculptural surface.

With 133 residential units, integrated landscaped terraces, and supporting facilities, the development presents a diversified experience of form and function. All of the service areas are located behind the sculptural screen and all rooms within each of the units have water-facing views. Continuous balconies along the façade blur the edge between exterior and interior, while floor-to-ceiling windows offer residents unblocked views. Exclusivity is enhanced with private lift access for each unit.

Weaving throughout the grounds of the project are vertical green walls, interlocking planters and local flora. The landscape culminates in an outdoor terrace at the tower podium, providing direct visual connection to the river. This landscaped podium roof and riverside terrace, adorned with swimming and spa pools, and outdoor decks, surround residents with a tropical garden ambiance. The Banyan Tree Riverside Residences builds upon an understanding of its local context, both architecturally and experientially, providing residents a stroke of timeless modernity.

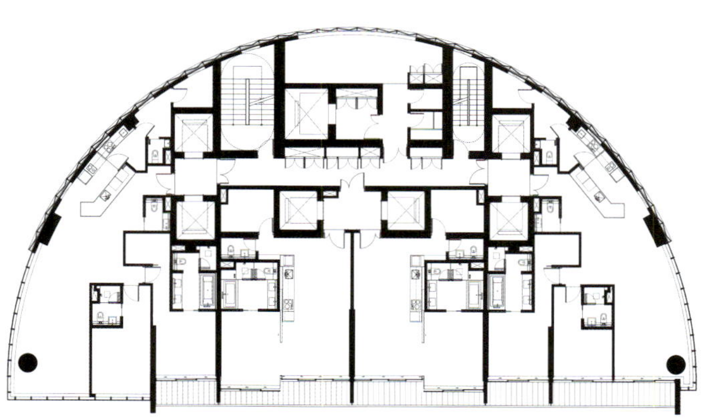

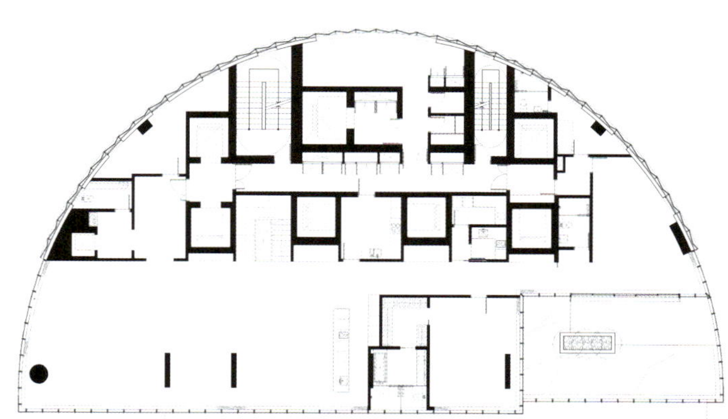

BAAN CHAOPRAYA

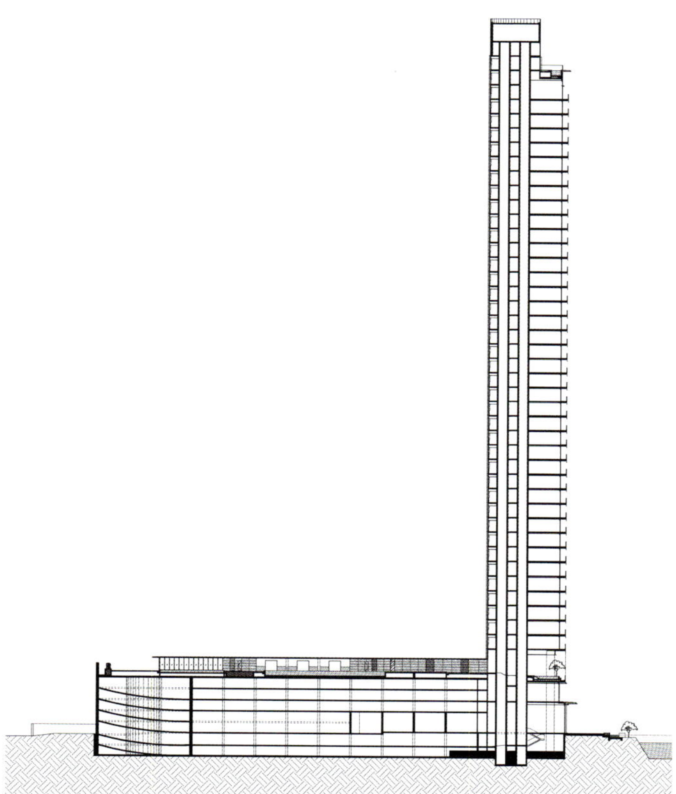

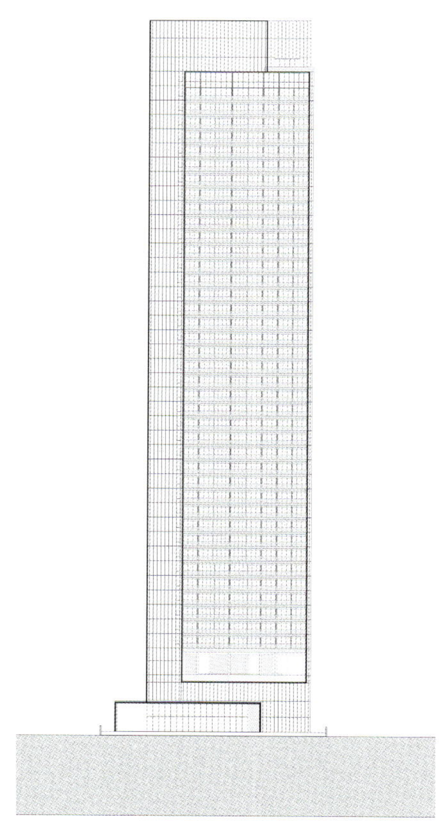

capri
capri
WISMA IMBI

CAPRI BUKIT BINTANG

Kuala Lumpur, Malaysia, 2015

Sitting within the vibrant and dense urbanity of Bukit Bintang, Capri by Fraser, a 43-story hotel, differentiates from Kuala Lumpur's common tower typology with its distinctive architectural approach. Rather than towering over a large anonymous parking podium, as is frequently encountered in Kuala Lumpur, the slender sculpted volume of Capri directly descends to ground level, creating an uninterrupted connection with the streets below.

As guests ascend, they are treated to increasingly open views of the city with the sky lobby and hotel facilities atop the tower offering panoramic vistas. The crown of the hotel is occupied by an outdoor infinity pool with views over the surrounding developments.

Functional elements such as circulation and accommodation receive careful consideration and design. The development's car park is hidden at the tower's rear, utilizing a vertical stacked mechanical structure to minimize the tower footprint and to allow for the main spaces of the program to be optimized along the main frontage.

In addition to the creation of an articulated architecture, the development transforms an adjacent drainage reserve into a street-side garden retreat—a quiet escape from the noise of the city. The entrance lobby, featuring natural wood accents and curated greenery, elevates a sense of refinement and arrival.

The building's main façade is not just visually striking but equally functional. Angular projecting architectural fins create rhythmic movement ascending the façade while providing sun shading, increasing the building's sustainability measures. This blend of form and function elevates Capri by Fraser from mere accommodation to a visual and experiential intervention within Kuala Lumpur's urban infrastructure.

Capri

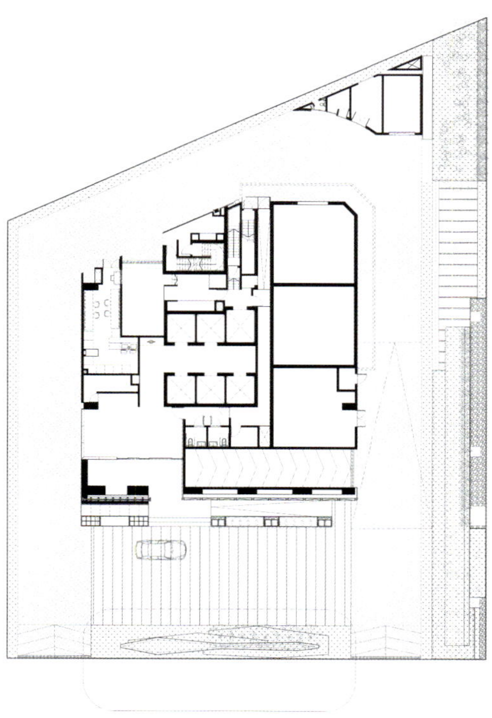

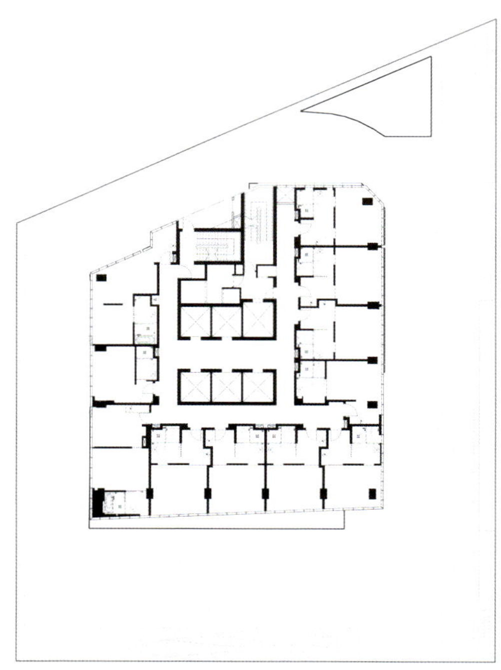

CAPRI BUKIT BINTANG

SAVYAVASA

Jakarta, Indonesia, 2017

Situated in the Dharmawangsa neighborhood of South Jakarta, a 3-hectare green expanse stands as a tribute to the area's Dutch colonial history, part of the Garden City Movement legacy. Responding to this historical canvas, SCDA aimed to sculpt a contemporary residential space while paying homage to the site's past.

The project comprises of a series of two-, three-, and four-bedroom apartments, distributed across three 40-story towers.

Emerging from the foliage, these structures sit within the parkland, while forming focal points for established vistas. Within the apartments, a longitudinal layout coupled with full height glazing ensures all living spaces and bedrooms have unobstructed views of the greenery against Jakarta's urban backdrop. Deep eaves guide residents onto expansive balconies spanning the façade, promoting an indoor-outdoor living ethos. The living and dining areas, flanking the tower footprint, feature double-height volumes and terraces, maximizing natural light penetration and ventilation.

Architectural fins and deep eaves articulate the façade, framing views and organizing these outdoor extensions of internal spaces. These design elements, reminiscent of the Dutch colonial dwellings, are adapted to a high-rise context, fostering a "Houses in the Sky" concept.

A design approach ensuring a gradual ascent to the elevated residential lobbies was adopted, providing a grand vantage towards the landscape. Amenities such as swimming pools and gyms are tucked below, leveraging the natural sloping terrain.

The use of natural finishes like timber and stone throughout the towers and common areas at ground level offer a tactile palette, blending with the landscape, thus crafting a modern residential enclave rooted in historical context.

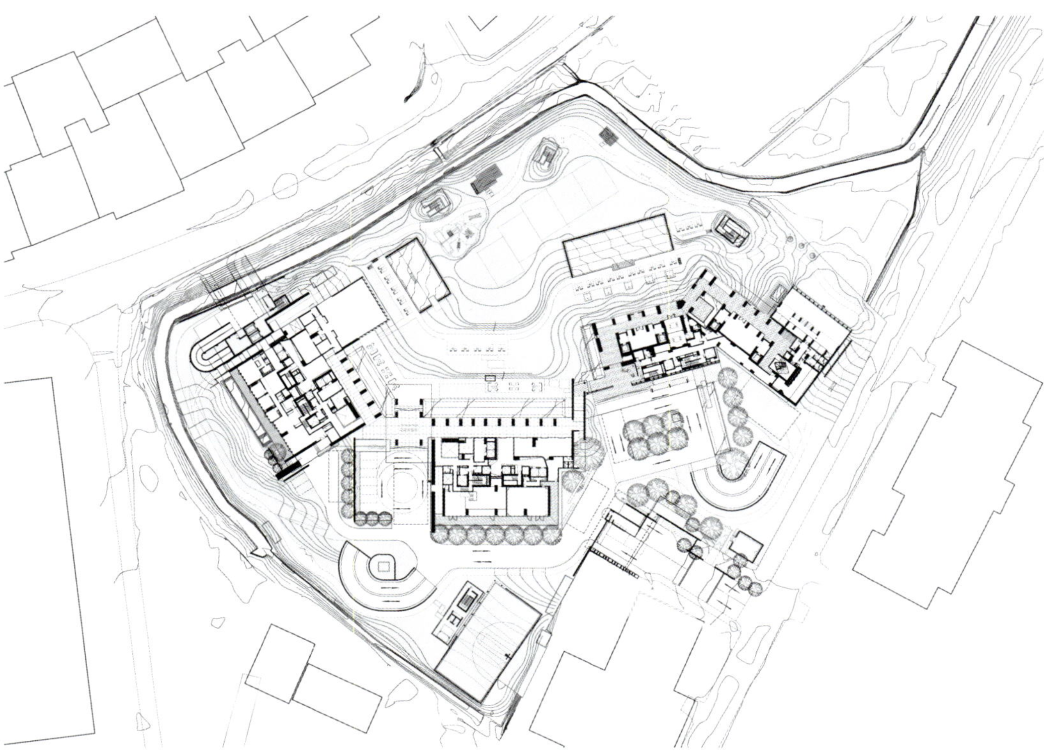

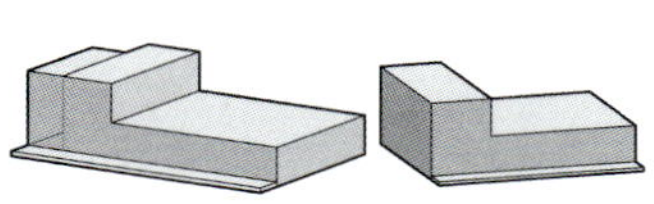

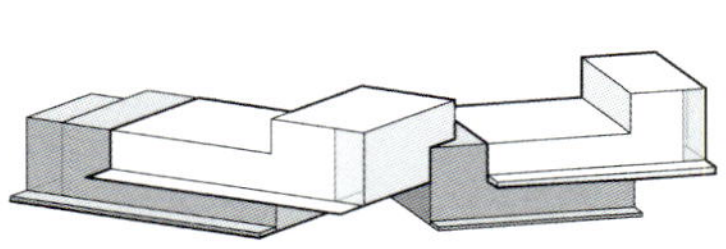

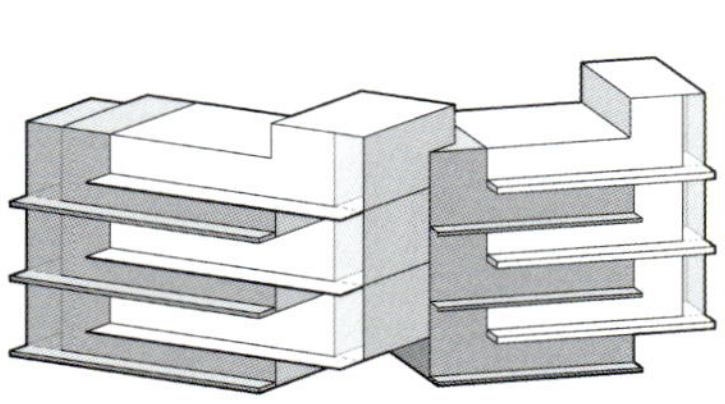

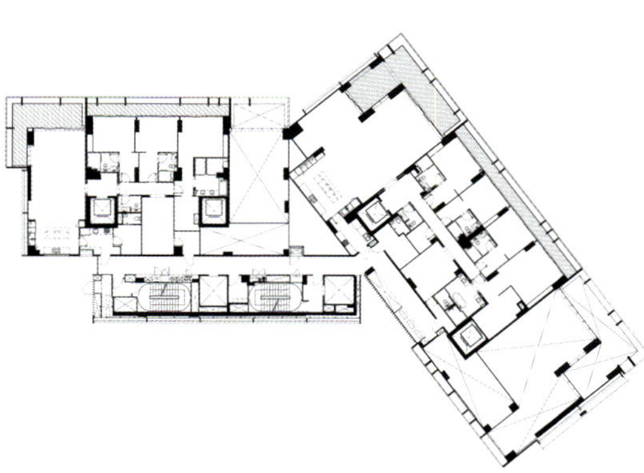

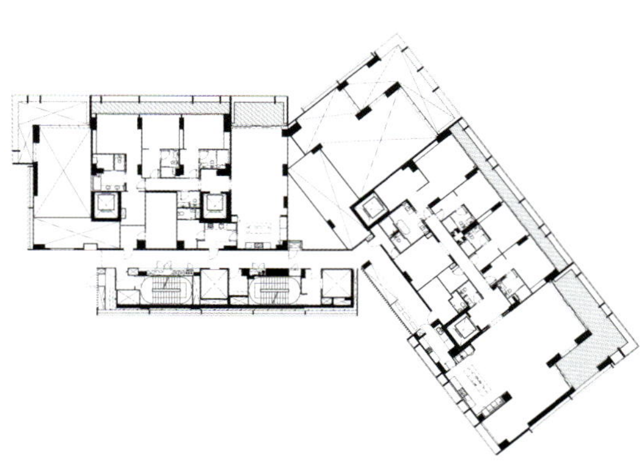

19 Nassim

19 NASSIM

Singapore, 2018

Set in lush tropical landscape, close to the UNESCO World Heritage Singapore Botanic Gardens, 19 Nassim is designed to take advantage of its location, embodying the concept of garden living. With access from the exclusive Nassim Hill residential enclave and visible from Napier Road, the address is a confident statement of understated luxury set within a tropical garden environment.

The site is perched on a steep incline and the design solution responds to the topography. The building is conceived as a floating volume with a continuous landscape plane that runs through. Residents and guests arrive at an elevated arrival court and descend a ceremonial stair, alongside cascading water features to the swimming pool deck fringed by lush landscaping.

All units have full-height glazing visually extending the interior into the exterior realm. Ground-floor apartments feature private patios that are screened by perimeter planting. Premium double-volume corner units with private lift access allow for generous double-height living spaces. The roof is activated by a residents' lounge, outdoor decks, and a wellness pool with views over Nassim Hill and Orchard Road.

The project's elegantly detailed façade is richly layered with screens that provide sun shading and privacy to the full-height windows and balconies that stretch across the volumes. Service areas of the units are provided with ventilation and lighting through courtyards that are placed in the deeper recesses of the volumes.

The development is an example of a bespoke and boutique residential space that embraces tropical architecture and redefines the approach to contemporary cosmopolitan living.

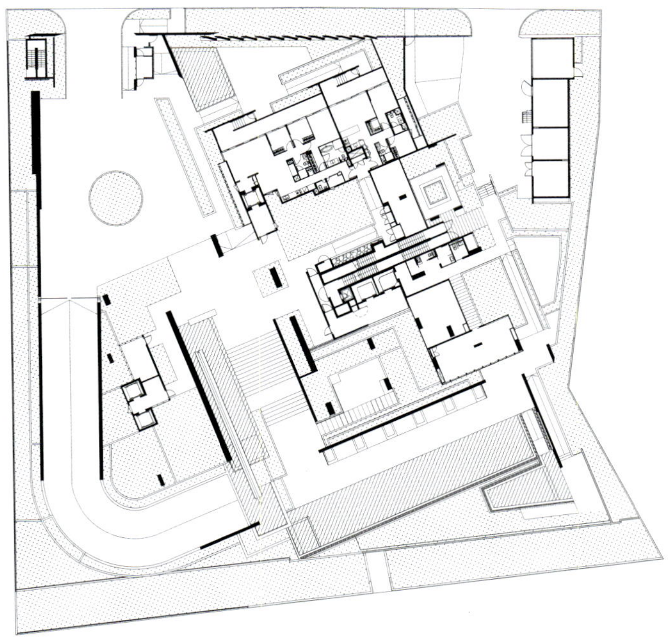

19 Nassim

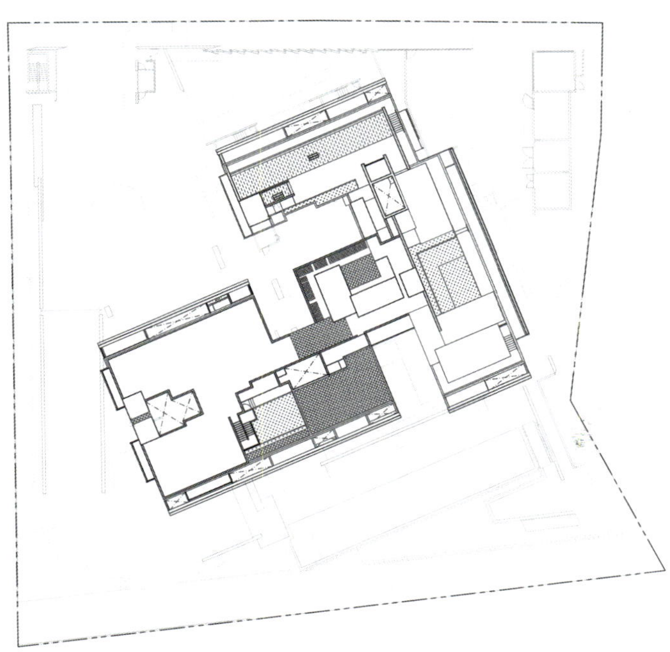

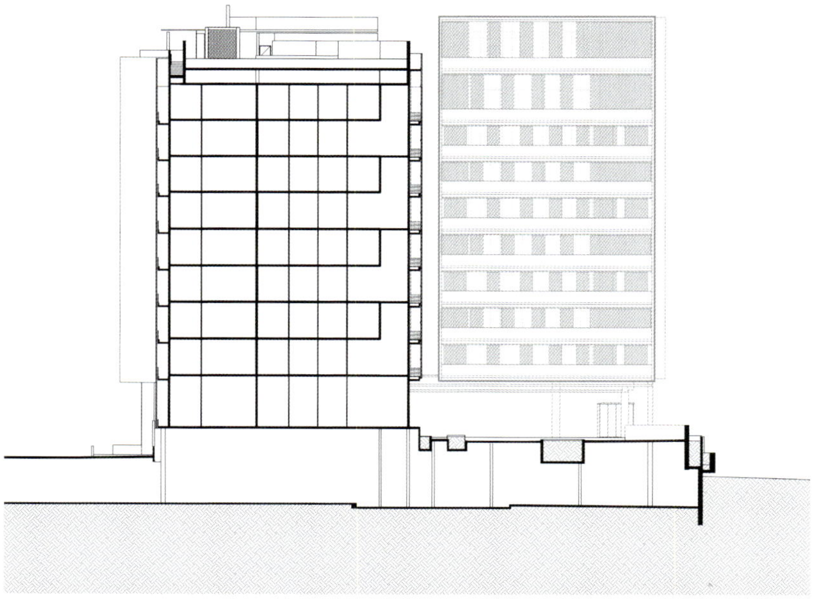

SKYTERRACE@ DAWSON

Singapore, 2009

SkyTerrace@Dawson represents a new generation of public housing in Singapore that embodies three key ideas: housing in a park, connectivity to surroundings and multi-generational living.

The project site is located in Dawson Estate with a public park running along its entire southern boundary. The precinct is composed of five residential 43-story towers and a four-story linear carpark podium.

Block planning takes advantage of the site's long north-and-south boundary by aligning the residential towers along this axis, maximizing the development's north-south exposure and limiting frontage to the strong western sun.

In response to the first two key ideas, the project site was planned to have direct connectivity on three sides to greenery. This green concept is further brought into the development by introducing lush planting on the ground plane that travels up the building façade in the form of green terracing, roof gardens, and landscaped sky terraces that span between the towers. The third design idea aims to reinforce the idea of multi-generational living and community building by providing the spatial framework for extended families to occupy interconnected loft units. These loft units are designed to combine a paired double-story four- or five-room unit with an elderly-friendly studio apartment unit. Each combined unit enjoys a double-height living room that is attached on the upper level to a loft space and connecting door to the adjacent studio unit.

The tower elevation design showcases the interlocking spaces that are created by the loft concept. Units are clearly defined by architectural edge fins that give a clear crisp silhouette to the towers as well as provide sun shading to the south-facing façade. The project features sustainable design technologies such as drip irrigation, rainwater harvesting, bio-retention basins, and solar energy systems, and is a Greenmark Platinum certified project.

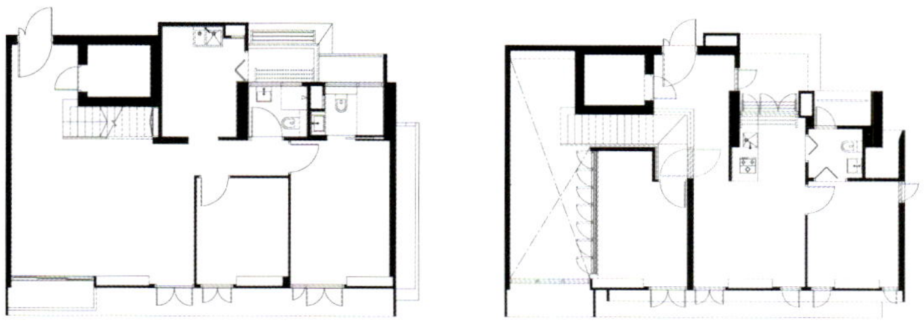

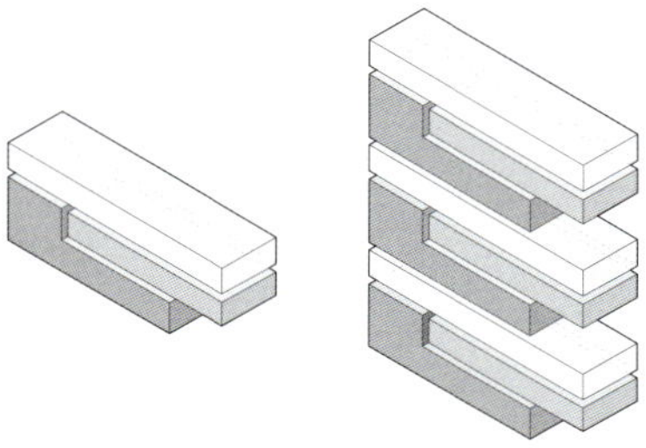

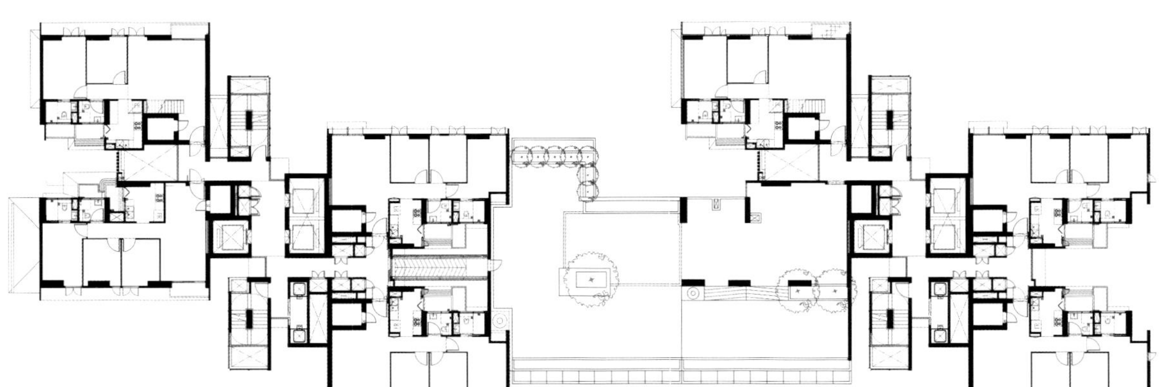

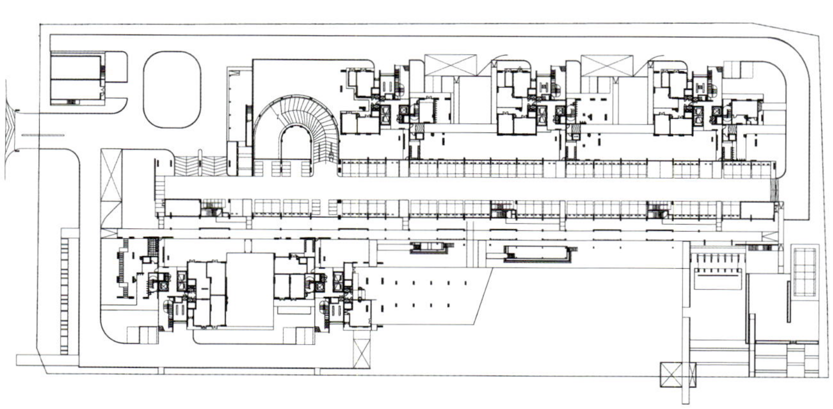

SKYTERRACE@DAWSON

OCT TIAN E BAO

Shenzhen, China, 2013

Adjacent to the scenic Tian E Lake in OCT Overseas Town and graced by the natural expanse of YanHanShan Park, the design approach centers on connection to the lake while establishing a distinct identity amidst the older neighboring structures.

A clean and glazed façade takes center stage, broken into smaller volumes with overlapping glass boxes. Vertical blade walls act as a backdrop, accentuating the crisp lines of the curtain wall. Aluminum screens, strategically placed, ensure privacy and sun shading on the east and west façade, contributing to a dynamic architectural composition.

The towers float above the landscaped ground plane, allowing garden courts and reflecting water bodies to merge with glazed lobbies, colonnaded covered decks and amenities. Units are oriented in a predominantly north-south orientation to ensure optimal daylight penetration in the winter months and views to the lake. Attention is paid to controlling heat transmission by the use of double-glazed low e-glass. Horizontal metal mesh fins provide sun shading on the southern façades while vertical trellises on the east and west gables provide additional protection from glare.

Tian E Lake, a cherished natural amenity, poses a unique challenge and opportunity. The lake's edges are delicately treated to retain their natural form, with layers of thoughtfully selected trees and shrubs blurring the boundaries between man-made and natural elements. Careful planning ensures public access to the lake while maintaining a balanced coexistence of residences with a sense of privacy. The outcome is a symphony: a harmonious blend of built and natural environments, and a seamless orchestration of new and existing elements.

OCT TIAN E BAO

OCT PARK
DEW LOUNGE
Domino's Pizza

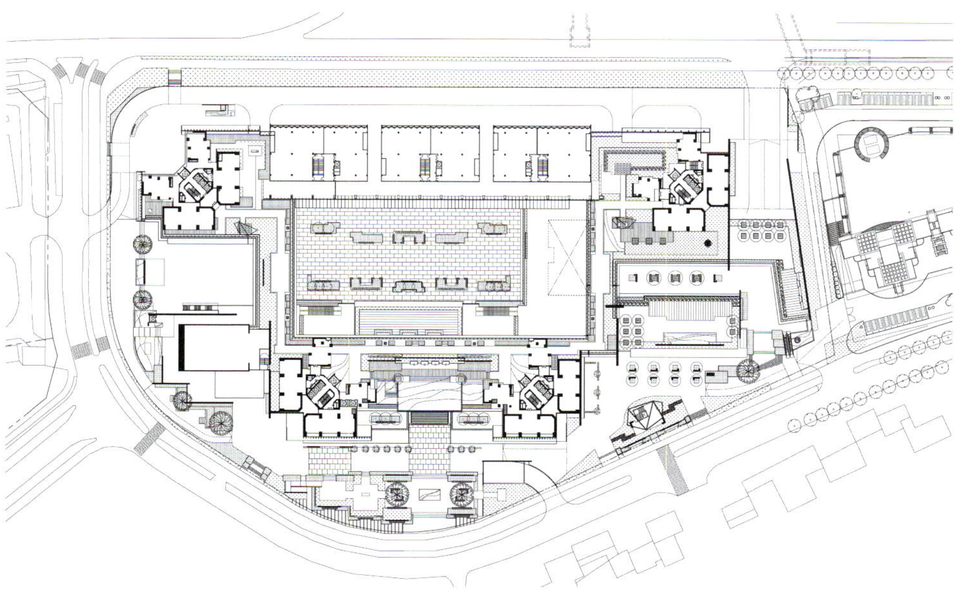

OCT PARK
3号门

THE SANYA EDITION

Hainan, China, 2017

Positioned along Hainan Island's tropical Haitang Bay coast, this expansive 19.5-hectare development redefines the conventional hotel concept. SCDA collaborated with the Ian Schrager team and Edition Hotels to conceptualize this project.

Beyond merely a hotel, the property includes privately-owned villas, conference facilities, and various leisure amenities around the private ocean—a man-made lagoon separated from the South China Sea by a pristine beach. The entry procession leads visitors through a meandering drive under arching rain trees, culminating at a towering 12-meter porte cochère and a dramatic 16-meter high arrival portal with a reflecting pool and tall bamboos framing ocean views.

Throughout, SCDA's design intertwines the ocean with architecture. The ocean promenade, in front of the hotel lobby, ascends in curved terraces, creating a green waterside amphitheater, following the site's topography.

The architectural façade serves a functional purpose beyond aesthetics. Aluminum screens address privacy along corridors, while the oceanfront façade employs light frames as the main articulation for each of the seven blocks, complemented by finely detailed glass balcony railings and privacy screens.

In response to Sanya's tropical climate, public spaces and corridors are naturally ventilated and opens up to the surrounding resort gardens. To address seasonal typhoon-driven rain, composite timber pivot screens were introduced at the edges of the podium, providing protection during adverse weather conditions.

Arranged in two rows, the villas are nestled into terraced terrain, ensuring that each unit had a picturesque view of the private ocean. This arrangement, coupled with existing site conditions, establishes an engaging terracing relationship between the two rows of villas, balancing individual privacy with unblocked views.

Smaller elements, such as food and beverage outlets, are placed along the private beach or perched directly above the ocean's waters, fostering a soft transition between indoor and outdoor spaces with timber decks and private pools.

EDITION

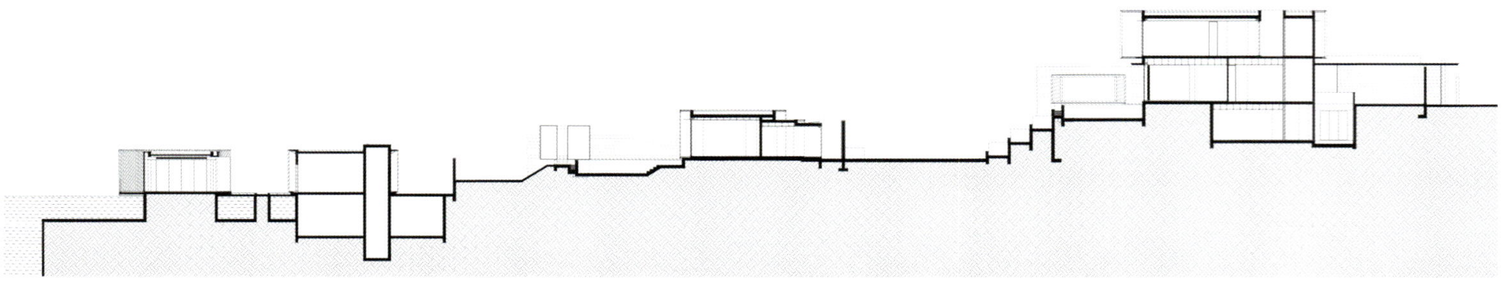

EDITION

LA CADIERE LAKESIDE CITY

Chengdu, China, 2020

La Cadiere Lake City emerges as a distinctive architectural ensemble in Chengdu's Yixin Lake district that intertwines residential, commercial, and cultural typologies.

Central to the development's design is the serene Yixin Lake, embraced by verdant gardens that blend with the urban fabric. Landscaped plazas and squares are positioned lakeside, offering users spaces for gathering, combining diverse functions within a singular gesture. Situated on the shores of the lake, the La Cadiere Art Center serves as the primary gateway to the development. This contemporary sculptural structure is characterized by its angular volumes and textured glass envelope, floating above a stepped public plaza. The focal point of La Cadiere Lake City is the Corporate Mansion Towers, sited to command panoramic views of the central lake and urban surroundings. The towers, formally simple, incorporate a nuanced composition of horizontal and vertical elements, forming a distinguishing backdrop to the lake.

Clad in silver aluminum paneling, arranged in a gridded configuration, the towers emanate a simple sophistication. Light silver low-energy glass complements the cladding, affording unobstructed views beyond. Architectural elements such as fins, fenestrations, and louver further define the exterior, imparting a sense of depth and character to the overall composition.

At ground level, the landscape meandering around the towers offers residents a natural retreat. The arrangement of courtyards, pavilions, and water features serves as an experiential entry point. Landscaped promenades extend to the central lawn, merging the interior and exterior programs.

The south zone landscape, reminiscent of an urban oasis, showcases interconnected courtyards and tiered gardens that provide secluded retreats for residents. Stepped landscaped terraces frame picturesque panoramas of Yixin Lake, while a monumental sculptural water feature mirrors the architectural forms. The soft-scape design, complemented by diverse flora, enhances the tranquil ambiance, epitomizing the seamless integration of architectural and natural elements at La Cadiere Lake City.

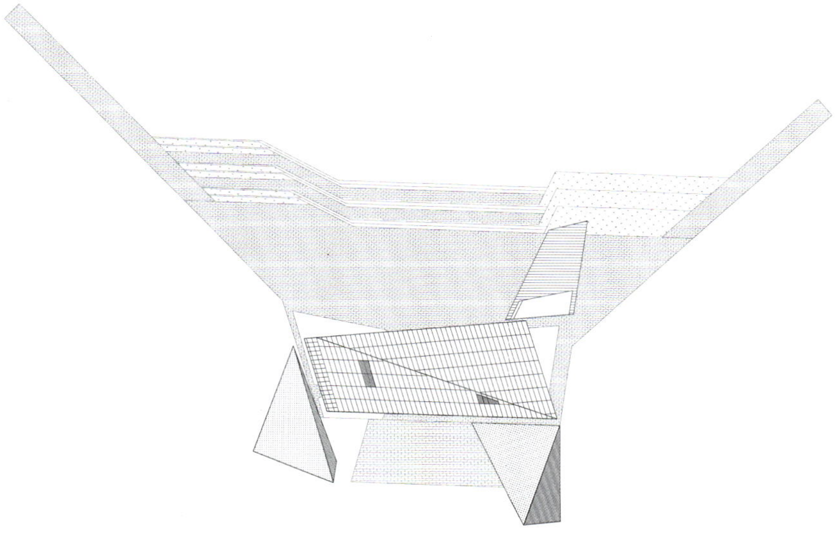

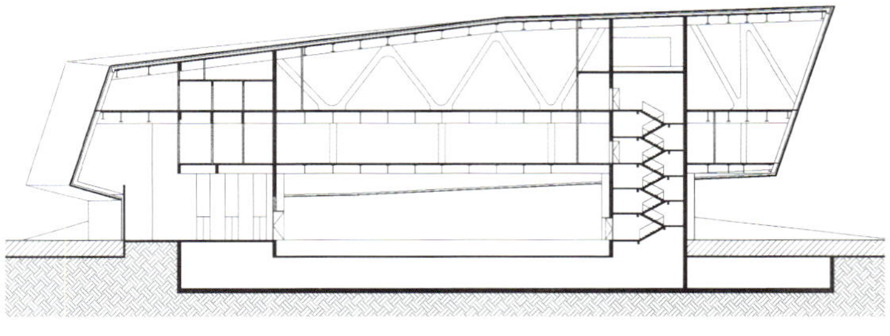

万科

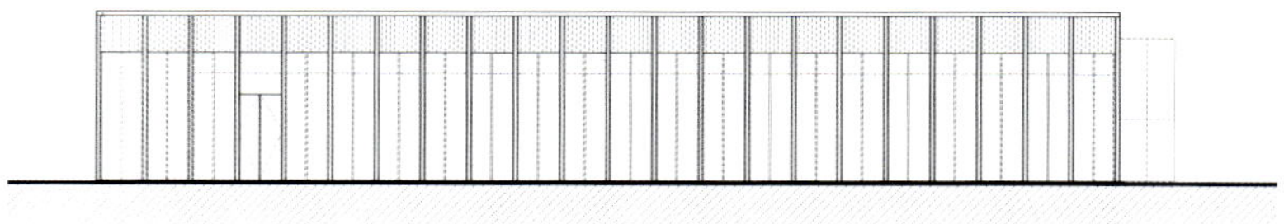

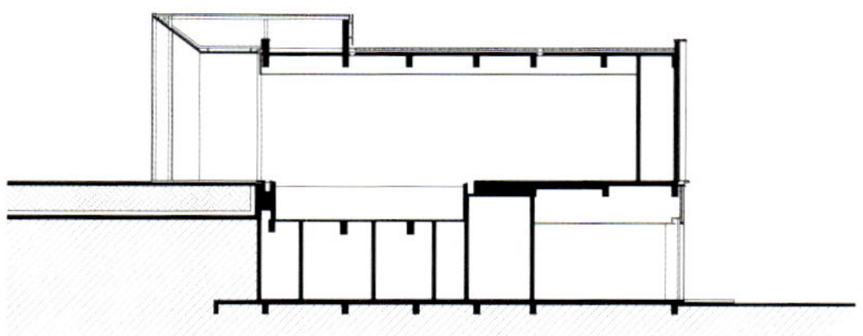

AMBER PARK

Singapore, 2018

Amber Park residences consists of three connected residential tower blocks that sit surrounding a large central landscaped lagoon. The towers were positioned to maximize surrounding views while striving to create a distinctive architectural dialogue for the area.

Connecting the development in a single gesture, the "Stratosphere," an elevated roof deck sitting 72 meters above sea level, spans across and connects the three towers through a series of bridges, paths, and gardens, offering unblocked views to the Singapore Straits.

The "Stratosphere" offers all residents a view of the nearby coastline and views to the city while releasing the pressure on ground floor facilities. A 600-meter jogging track winds through a series of landscape planters and water features culminating in framed views to the sea beyond.

The development is approached through a grand arrival court which links to the main central axis of the communal landscape lagoon. A 25-meter sculptural water feature forms a gateway to view the folding, overlapping geometries of the pool, pavilions and landscape which culminates in the sculptural "folded form" of the residents' clubhouse. A series of "archipelago" deck and terrace spaces sit within the large form pool, offering a variety of spaces to relax and retreat. The three-dimensional landscape curate views to minimize the impact of the surrounding tower massing.

The development transforms at night where the "Stratosphere" is lit along the length of its geometry, through integrated linear lighting, creating an abstract skyline, distinctive within its context. The balance of architecture and landscape conceived holistically creates a clear identity.

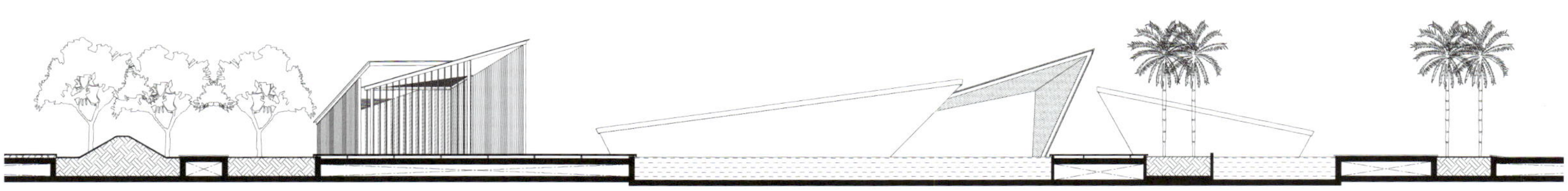

AMBER PARK

AMBER PARK

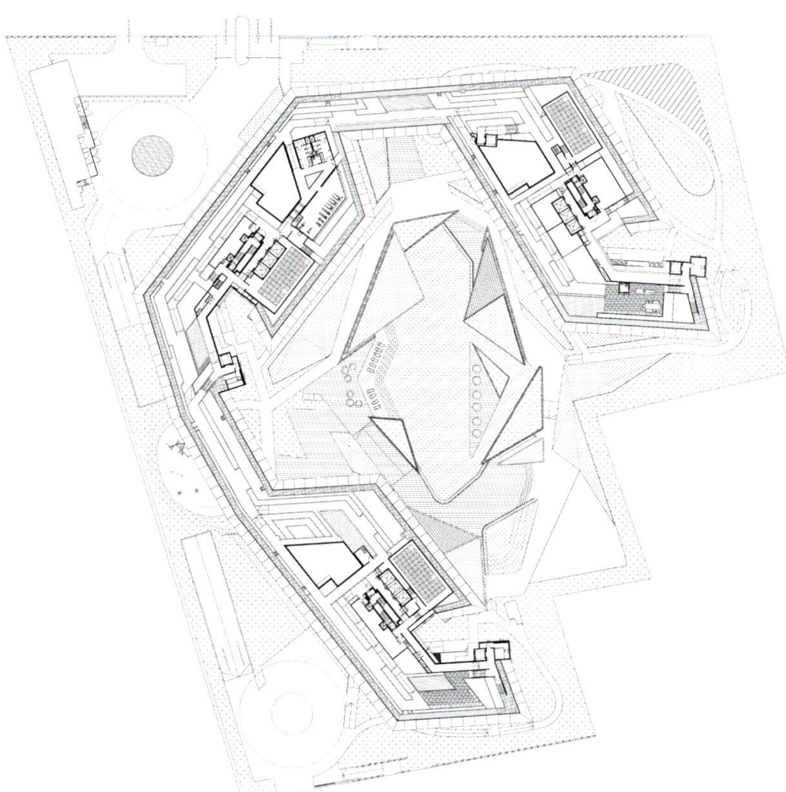

RIVIÈRE

Singapore, 2018

The Rivière sits along a prominent curve of the Singapore River, amidst a historically rich setting of early 20th century warehouses. The development comprises of two 36-story residential towers, a four-story service apartment podium and three conserved warehouses.

On arrival, residents and visitors are greeted by a plaza, an area of urban significance that imbues a sense of the river and the three different components of the development. A public thoroughfare maintains pedestrian connectivity between Jiak Kim Street and the Singapore River, allowing continuous access to the river promenade.

The design and position of the towers ensure unobstructed views towards Orchard Road to the north and Marina Bay to the south. This spatial arrangement not only maximizes the scenic vistas but also minimizes solar heat gain by orienting the buildings predominantly in the north and south direction—a practical design solution for tropical climates.

The façade design is a critical component of Rivière's architectural narrative. The northeast façade features vertical fins providing sun shading while allowing residents to enjoy the river views. These fins also contribute to defining a vertically dominant façade expression, extending to form a distinctive crown for the development.

Contrastingly, the north-west and south-east façade introduce a warmer aspect with deep overhanging balconies enveloped in timber-look fins. These balconies provide residents with outdoor spaces to enjoy river views, embodying a softer, tactile aesthetic that engages the surrounding river ambiance.

The service apartment block continues the undulating ridgeline of the conserved warehouse, with a façade interplay of steel and timber-look elements forming a contemporary grid. This design echoes the intricate detailing found in old riverside warehouse, providing a modern rendition of the area's industrial past.

Rivière extends beyond being a residential enclave by ensuring urban connectivity, creating a public access corridor from Jiak Kim Street to the riverside promenade and Jiak Kim Bridge. This thoughtful design gesture promotes a seamless interface between the private residential realm and the public urban milieu, contributing to the holistic living experience the development aims to offer.

RIVIÈRE

FRASERRESIDENCE
RIVIÈRE
FRASERRESIDENCE
RIVER PROMENADE-SINGAPORE

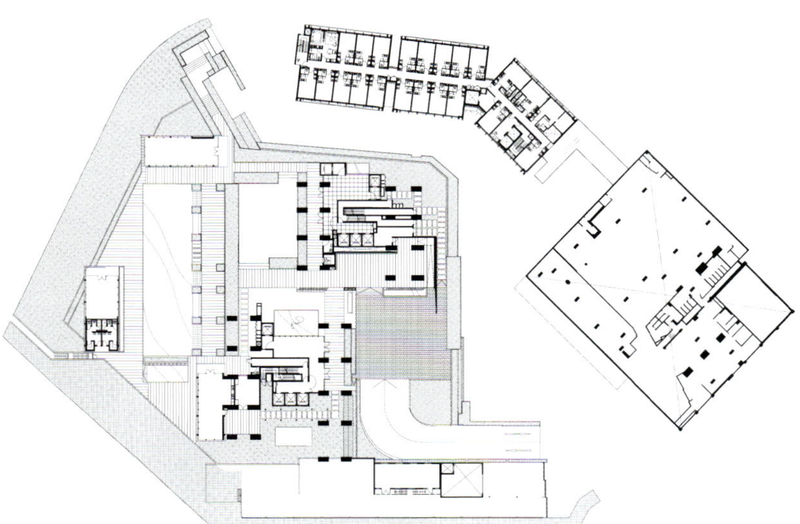

RIVIÈRE

STUDIO M
INTERCONTINENTAL

IHG ROBERTSON QUAY

Singapore, 2013

The Intercontinental Robertson Quay is a 226-room urban hotel situated in the historic Robertson Quay precinct along the Singapore River. It is a reconstruction of an earlier hotel built in 1999.

The architecture is reconceptualized as a collection of volumes with deliberate yet subtle shifts in geometry, clad in glass curtain wall of differing reflectivity and complemented with vertical sun screens.

With the increasing prominence of Robertson Quay as a dining and lifestyle hub along the Singapore River, SCDA's response is to cater to this growing segment by introducing fresh food and beverage (F&B) concepts and commercial spaces into the hotel's retail podium and incorporating outdoor dining around the perimeter of the hotel.

These dining and lifestyle concepts occupy large outdoor terraces on every floor of the retail podium and a lush pool deck on the fourth story podium roof. Every terrace overlooking the Singapore River affords generous views of the Central Business District (CBD) skyline and beyond.

The original hotel lobby at ground level is elevated to the fourth story to free up the podium for retail and F&B outlets. All existing hotel common areas and guestrooms have been reimagined and redesigned. The hotel lobby, lounge, and meeting facilities are conceptualized as residential living spaces. Guest rooms have full height floor-to-ceiling glass to maximize views and connection to the exterior. This redevelopment also involves refurbishing the Singapore River promenade along Robertson Quay. The introduction of a face-lifted Quayside retail podium fronted by a tree-lined pedestrianized promenade is envisioned to complement timber decked platforms and outdoor dining areas, catering to a vibrant riverfront precinct.

INTERCONTINENTAL
STUDIO M

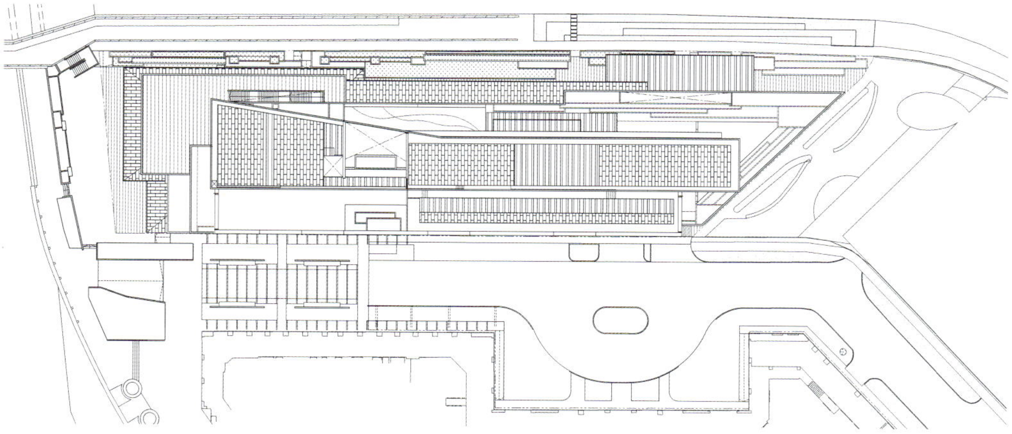

INTERCONTINENTAL.

INTERCONTINENTAL.
SINGAPORE ROBERTSON QUAY

INTERCONTINENTAL
Alexandra Rd
Outram Rd
New Bridge Rd
Upp Pickering St

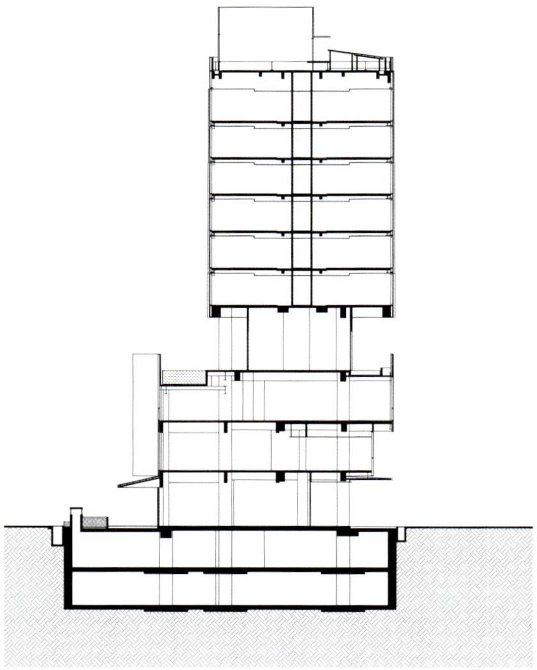

abc artisan boulangerie co.
DABBAWALLA

QUAYSIDE
the QUAYSIDE

IHG ROBERTSON QUAY

THE LALU

Nanjing, China, 2018

The Lalu Nanjing is situated on the confluence of Han Zhong Men DaJie, the main east-west artery of Nanjing and the banks of the Yangtze, nestled within a green belt park that runs alongside the east bank of the river. This prominent position allows for uninterrupted views, both directly across the water and diagonally along the Yangtze's landscaped banks.

The design solution is a conceptual gateway that celebrates the strong axial relationship of the project site to the city and its unique location on the banks of the Yangtze.

The main components of the development are placed as an extension of this axis, paying tribute to the traditional Chinese imperial and courtyard architectural planning principles of axial movement and symmetry. The groupings of the architectural components shape outdoor gardens and water courts that are composed along and adjacent to this central spine. Arrival and movement through the hotel are experienced as a journey through a series of unfolding internal and external spaces, culminating in a large landscaped garden that merges visually with the Yangtze.

The hotel component is placed in the most central position with vistas across the river and along its landscaped banks. The hotel is divided into two wings that form a gateway, crowned by a connecting linear landscaped platform.

The office and residential towers complete the architectural composition on the north-east and south-east corners respectively by embracing two large central landscaped courtyards. The hotel, residential, and office towers are placed on a retail podium that extends over the site and blends into the surrounding landscape.

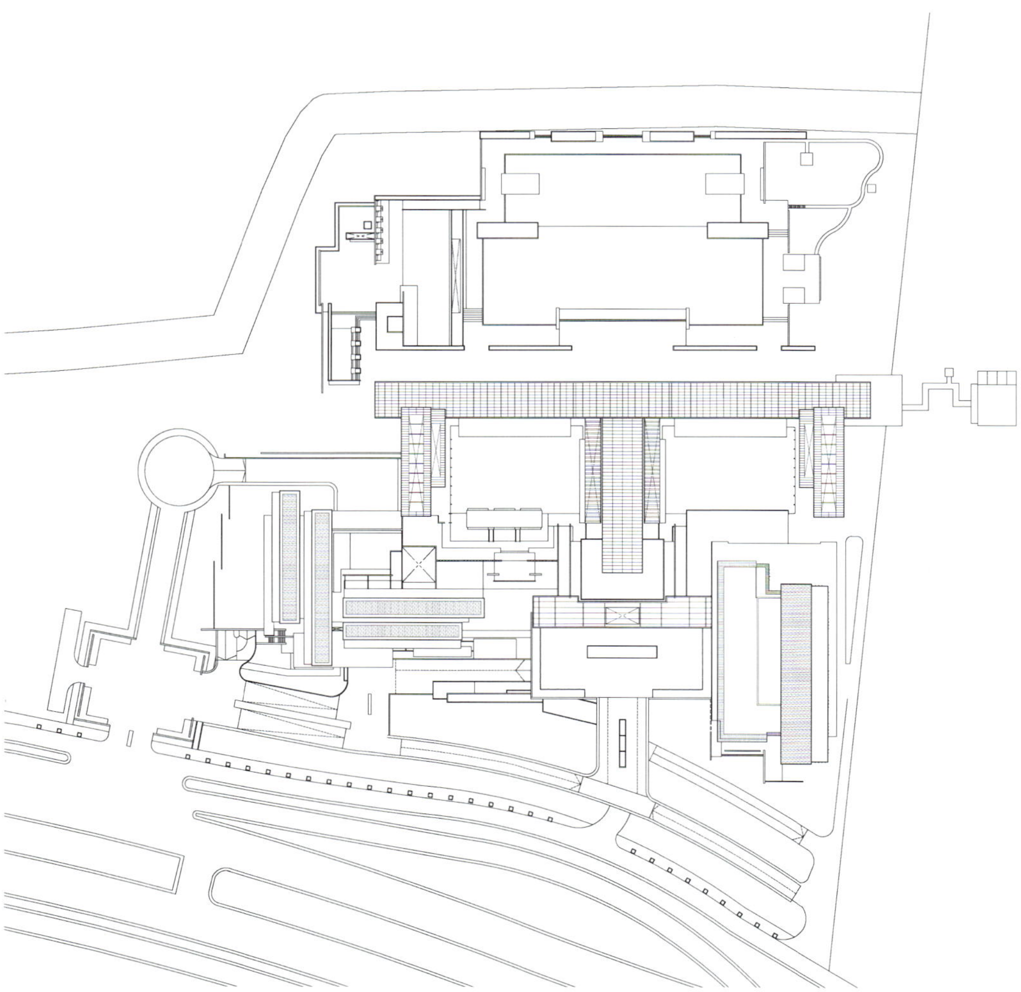

VANKE HANGZHOU

Hangzhou, China, 2017

Situated near West Lake, Xixi National Wetland Park and Qinglong River, this residential development prioritizes tranquility, offering residents a place of contemplation and refuge.

The project comprises of 11 residential towers of varying configurations, arranged in a predominantly north-south orientation. Towers are strategically positioned to frame open spaces, landscaped views and an offering of recreational activities within the residential area.

A formal entry pavilion is located on the southern periphery of the project. Lined pathways and covered galleries which extend between towers, before culminating at a sunken courtyard framed by large cascading water walls and reflecting pools. Surrounding this courtyard is the residents' clubhouse with a heated indoor swimming pool and residents' lounge. The design aims to facilitate ease and clarity of movement and creates a sense of place within the large residential compound. The dynamic architectural forms and façade articulation of the 11 residential towers serve as an urban catalyst for rejuvenating the surroundings while maintaining simplicity and uniformity.

The collection of towers, differing in unit layout and orientation are unified by a consistent façade language. The façade identifies with a holistic approach—incorporating a repetitive system of horizontal and vertical surfaces, balancing proportion and detail—breaking down the length of the towers to more balanced proportions. The material selection presents a pure white palette, integrating white aluminum paneling alongside monolithic stone cladding to create a clean canvas and pure spatial relationships.

The blending of these architectural elements enhances user experience, celebrating light and shadow, texture and experience.

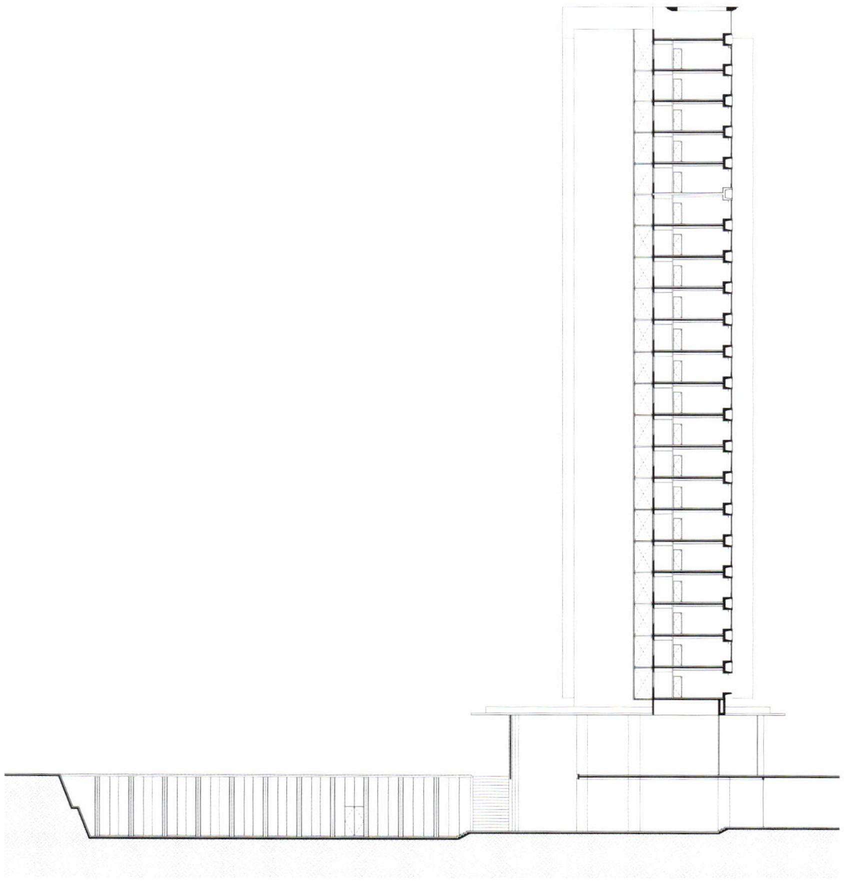

JUMEIRAH RESIDENCES

Dubai, UAE, 2024

Sited in the energetic Dubai International Financial District, this iconic project forms a distinct addition to the city skyline with its unique architecture and the curated experiences it provides for its inhabitants.

Rising 240 meters into the sky, the dual towers form a dialogue with the adjacent twin Emirates towers, while opening key vistas to eminent Dubai landmarks such as the Burj Khalifa, the Museum of the Future, and the Dubai Frame.

Each tower capitalizes on the specialty of its units—one tower features modules with double volumes and an interplay of space, creating mansions in the sky, while the other provides each unit with ample balconies, integrated across its façade. Articulated screens, flourishing landscape, and intricate balconies offer privacy and respite for residents. The rhythm of each elevation pauses at certain levels, expanding into dramatic sky terraces equipped with pools, gymnasiums, and charming spaces, allowing the tower to open up towards views of the surrounding city.

Sitting between the bases of the towers, carefully composed clubhouse masses provide key amenities. The negative space between towers thus serves to unify the two components, with club programs woven through carefully hidden support spaces, enabling the clubhouse to provide unparalleled levels of comfort and sophistication that will rival a luxury hotel.

While each tower provides a distinct grade of experience and product, the individual parts of the development seamlessly synthesize, orchestrating a synergy which derives opportunities from design challenges—therefore allowing the architectural whole to be greater than the sum of its parts.

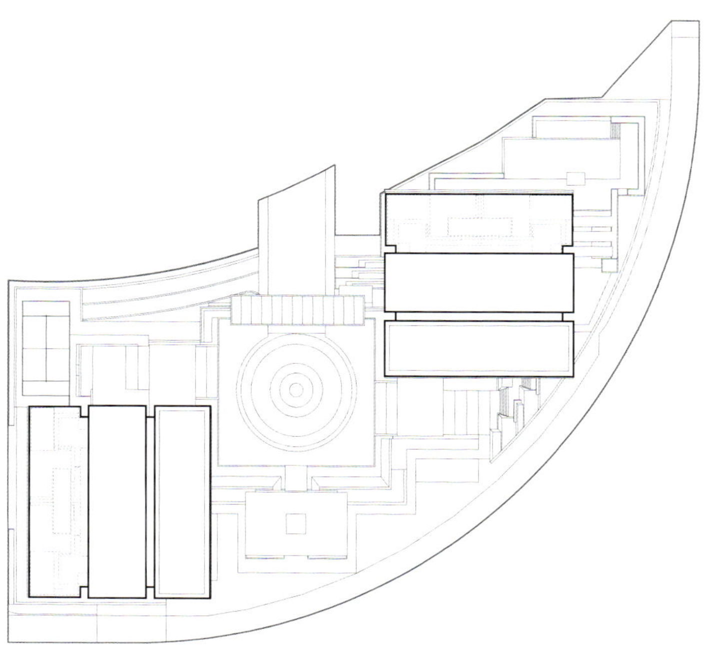

JUMEIRAH
RESIDENCES
EMIRATES TOWERS

MATTEL SHENZHEN

Shenzhen, China, 2020

Located in the foothills of Maluan Mountain with views of ShaTouJiao Sea to the east and Wutong Mountain to the south, SCDA's design solution embodies strong architectural geometries and a formal composition of elements.

Three distinct towers—office, residential, and hotel—are placed in opposing corners of the site to minimize overlooking and to allow maximum daylight penetration into the podium levels. The tower footprints and podium edges are purposefully angled to respond to the site geometries and arranged to maximize distances between each tower. The resultant composition creates an active interplay of sculpted forms and spatial hierarchies.

To connect the northern and southern plots, the hotel tower on the northern plot and the office tower on the south-east are linked by an overhanging wellness deck.

The vertical arrangement of the podium spaces responds closely to the existing site levels. The southern plot is divided into two; the eastern half raised to link the public road, naturally forms a private garden deck while the western half steps down and connects with a large urban plaza, adjacent to lush greenery and cascading water features.

The ground level of the two towers at the southern plot is kept open as a landscaped deck, forming a continuous outdoor public space, interacting with the green buffer on its western perimeter. Through layering of greenery, hardscape, and water features, meaningful spaces were crafted on the ground floor for both residents and the public.

The project fully exploits attributes of the site and makes a significant contribution to the urban realm by the creation and layered insertion of multiple public and semi-public decks and plazas.

MATTEL SHENZHEN

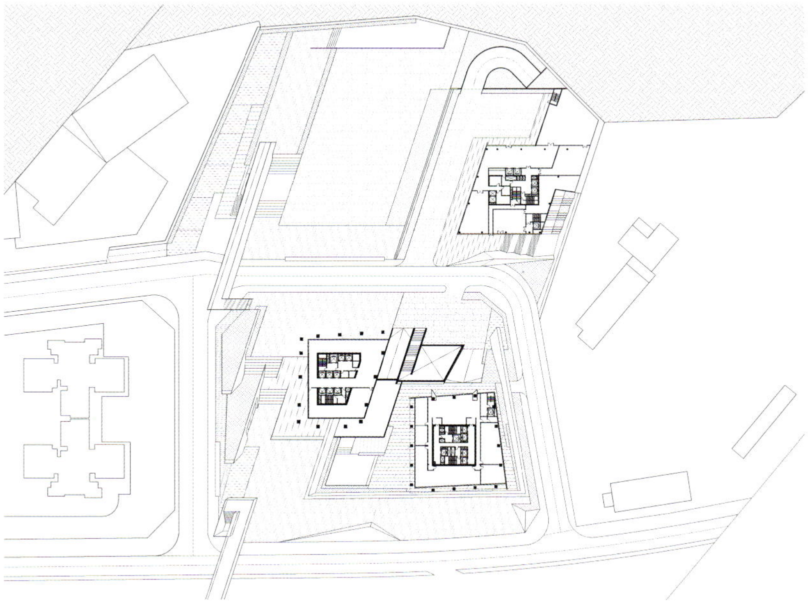

VANKE DAXIANG

Suzhou, China, 2017

The Daxiang residential development comprises of 18 14-story towers and 268 four-story duplexes, covering a total area of approximately 125,000-square meters. It is located in the eastern suburbs of Suzhou, adjacent to the Tianping Mountain Forest Park and the Taihu Lake Scenic Area. The development stretches along a meandering river with views to the mountains beyond.

Gradually rising in mass from the villas, the apartment blocks are arrayed in a north-south orientation and interspersed by linear landscaped gardens and parks. The low-rise villas encompass duplex units, utilizing internal volume and space while limiting building footprint.

The human scale of the villas evolves into the taller linear apartment towers, aligned to minimize sun shading. The interlocking façade of the towers are composed of external double-volume terraces, which stagger across the full height of the towers, visually expanding the interior space.

The use of materiality responds to scale with the low-rise villas using a warm palette of light "stone," silver louvers and timber inserts, materials echoed in the surrounding natural landscape. The towers use a combination of light silver aluminum trim edging with high reflectance glass panels creating a monolithic balcony form.

A large central courtyard with cantilevered gallery building sits centrally within the arrangement of the tower blocks, bringing light and ventilation to amenity spaces below and a focus of activity to the development. The interplay of textured stone walls and green hedges throughout the development creates a warm, harmonious base for the architecture of the towers and villas to sit upon.

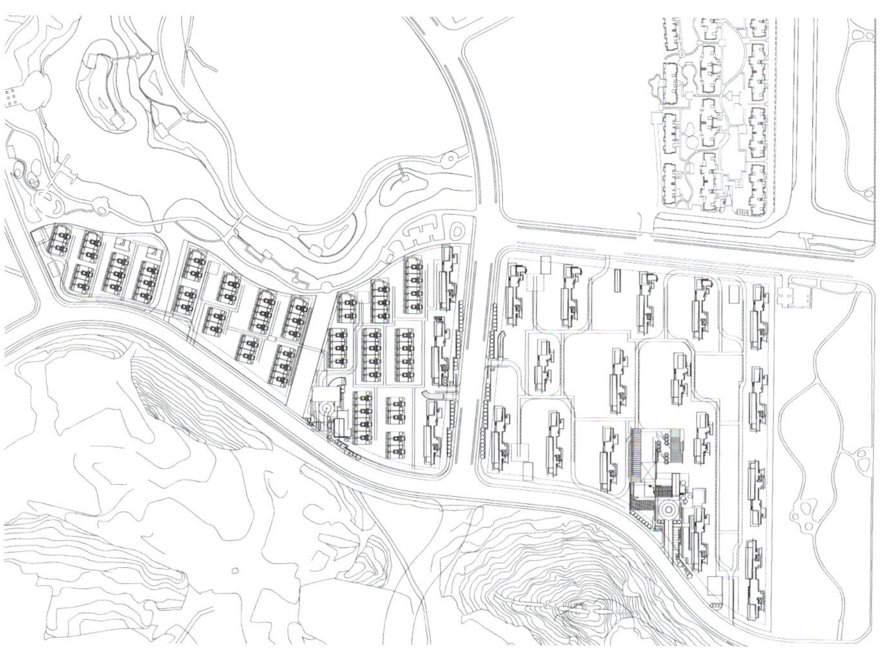

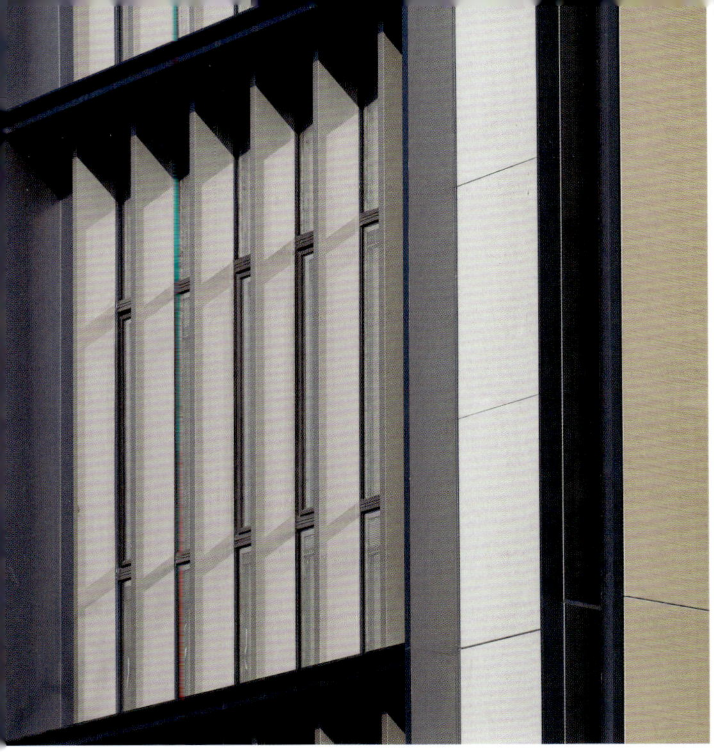

OUE
WN Gallery

OUE DOWNTOWN

Singapore, 2019

Situated along Shenton Way—the city's historic financial artery—the development strives to revitalize an existing commercial development, forging a strong connection to the CBD, while enhancing a sense of both place and passage.

The design transforms an ageing late-modernist office complex balancing a reverence for its original form with a new strong contemporary expression. Verticality of the tower, expressed through slender glass and aluminium façade elements, sit rooted by a robust horizontal plinth housing the commercial mall that anchors the composition. The tower form is dissected into its parts by deep reveals lined with timber cladding reinforcing the interplay of load and lightness.

The reveals, an homage to the original form, light gently at night to offer a respite from the prevalent conventional glass tower typology. A unifying podium base stitches together the disparate buildings with a cohesive tectonic language, creating a harmonious yet assertive urban ensemble, revitalising the streetscape.

A large above grade car park volume wrapped in a veil of undulating perforated panels connects to an over ground link bridge connecting pedestrian flow and creating an elevated street. Large volumes subtracted from the podium base create street atria, transitional spaces managing fluid movement and circulation between the varying programs.

This synthesis of structure, circulation, and materiality repositions OUE Downtown not merely as a retrofit, but as an urban actuator—renegotiating Shenton Way's architectural legacy within Singapore's evolving urban grid.

OUEDOWNTOWN

OUE DOWNTOWN

OUE DOWNTOWN
OUE

OUE

OUE DOWNTOWN

SEVENTY

Ahmedabad, India, 2013

The overall identity and façade of Seventy is that of timeless volumetric minimalism. Standing 70 meters tall, the project consists of 70 apartments with double-volume high-ceiling living rooms, private lifts, large outdoor balcony decks, and corner master bedrooms with full height windows that open up to two sides. Every unit is conceived as a villa in the sky. The interlocking spatial configuration of the master bedrooms and living spaces gives the design its distinctive architectural profile and expression.

Frameless curtain wall systems are employed to give the building an understated, clean expression. Subtle horizontal sun shading fins and vertical trims are added for functionality and added textural depth. The vertical trims at the master bedroom façade act as privacy screens, while allowing for maximum light penetration. Projecting horizontal fins help to shade the living spaces with minimal obstruction to views. Kitchens and back of house functions are located adjacent to inward oriented service cores to maintain a clean and uncluttered outward facing tower façade.

On arrival, residents enter into a large ceremonial drop-off court in the center of the site, anchored by a central water feature, defined with landscape feature walls, perimeter planting and flanked by two high-ceilinged grand lobbies. At roof level, spanning between the two residential towers sits "The Cloud," where residents enjoy a 15-meter lap pool with panoramic views, garden spaces, games room, gymnasium, and a club lounge. Seventy, as a whole, elevates the urban skyline of Ahmedabad's central commercial district.

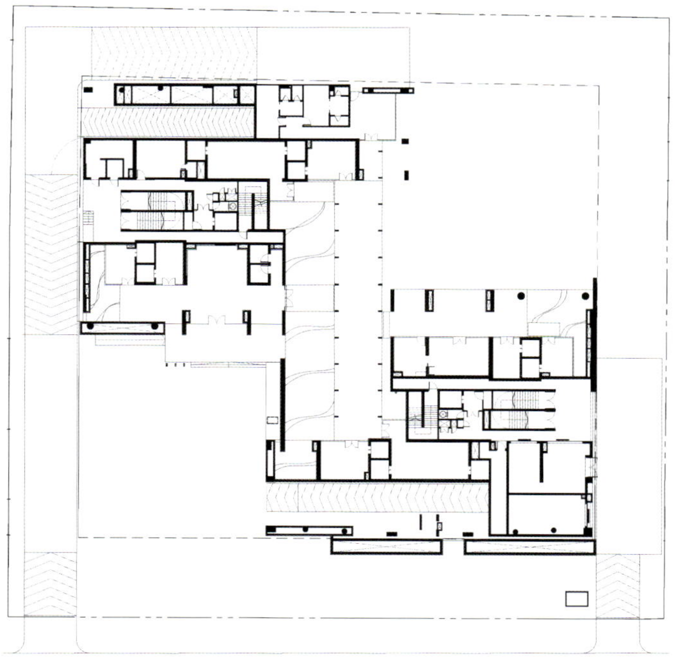

bSafal signature residences

JUHU BEACH RESIDENCE

Mumbai, India, 2023

Juhu Beach Residence sits in the eastern flank of Mumbai, directly on the stretch of Juhu coastline renowned for its scenic beauty and vibrant atmosphere.

The architecture is distinctively simple and modern, incorporating clean lines and edges, featuring large overhanging planes juxtaposed against pure glass volumes. Sun shading fins and screens add a layer of detail to the overall composition of the architectural expression. A predominantly timber-textured material palette is chosen to impart a warm residential patina to the façade.

The estate consists of five stacks of abutting residential towers oriented to directly face the Arabian Sea. All apartment units have large double-volume living rooms, master bedrooms and expansive cantilevered balconies that open up to unblocked sea views. Occupying the upper levels, penthouse units accessible by private lift enjoy their own private roof decks.

The entire ground plane is lifted to enhance privacy and provide sea views over the adjacent beach. Anchoring the grounds of the estate is a large manicured and tree-lined formal lawn, creating a private and tranquil resort sanctuary for residents. Surrounding the apartment towers, lush flora forms smaller intimate spaces that allow residents to feel deeply connected to nature. A large clubhouse with specialty dining, wellness, and sports facilities is located beneath the lifted podium.

The north-east corner of the landscape deck features a residents' club, with its distinct folded architectural roof. Adjacent to the club lounge, a sunset deck, gathering spaces with beverage services, and an infinity pool, frames views of the horizon.

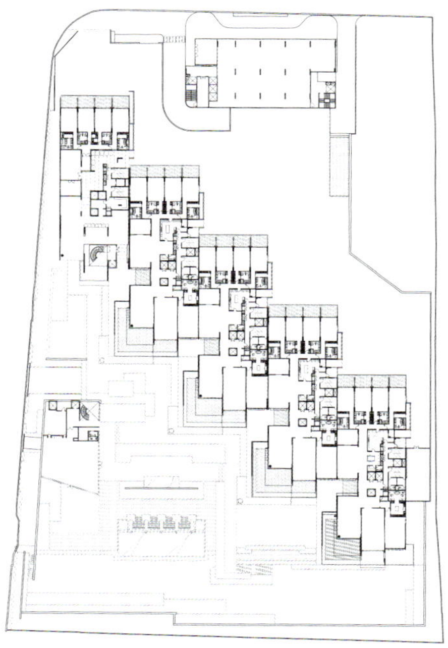

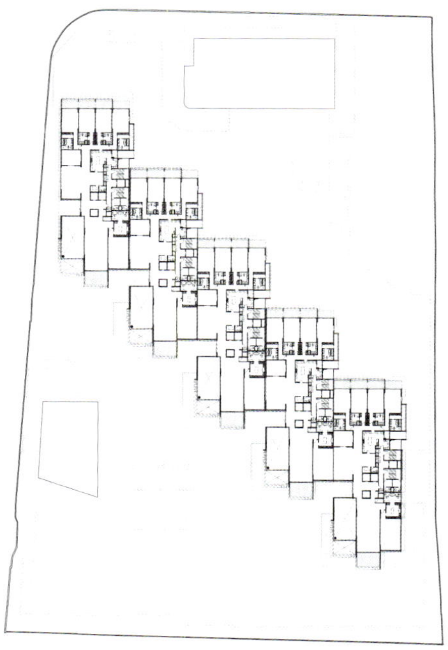

JUHU BEACH RESIDENCE

ALIBAUG LODHA

Alibaug, India, 2023

Located an hour from Mumbai by ferry, Alibaug is conceived as a residential oasis for city dwellers. Situated between lush mangroves and the sea, the development taps on its proximity to abundant nature to provide a respite from urbanity.

With a focus on reconnecting residents with their natural surroundings, much of the existing landscape elements skirting the periphery of the site were retained, and an ecological boardwalk through the well-established mangroves was introduced. These elements complement the man-made lake which serves as the critical spine to the master plan from which all programs radiate out from.

A retail promenade engages and activates the water's edge, while residential towers sit atop a landscaped podium, buffering the residents from the public realm. The radial orientation of the towers not only respond to the site's existing elements, they also ensure that overlooking between towers is reduced, allowing for unobstructed views towards the sea.

On the opposite bank, detached homes and town houses have a choice of a waterfront frontage or views to the mangrove forest.

The low-density dwellings have been lifted from the ground, affording better views and greater privacy. The seamless integration between the natural and built environment continues with an elevated green walkway penetrating the townhouse precinct, providing residents with direct access to the development's amenities, chief among which is the clubhouse with its food and beverage, leisure, function, and wellness offerings. As a central hub of activity, the clubhouse is highly visible from all parts of the development, anchoring the lake with its iconic design.

A grand arrival plaza next to the clubhouse serves as a vantage point towards the development. One traverses a lushly landscaped driveway before opening to this vista. This journey has been intentionally crafted to evoke a strong sense of arrival and to mediate between the development and what lies beyond.

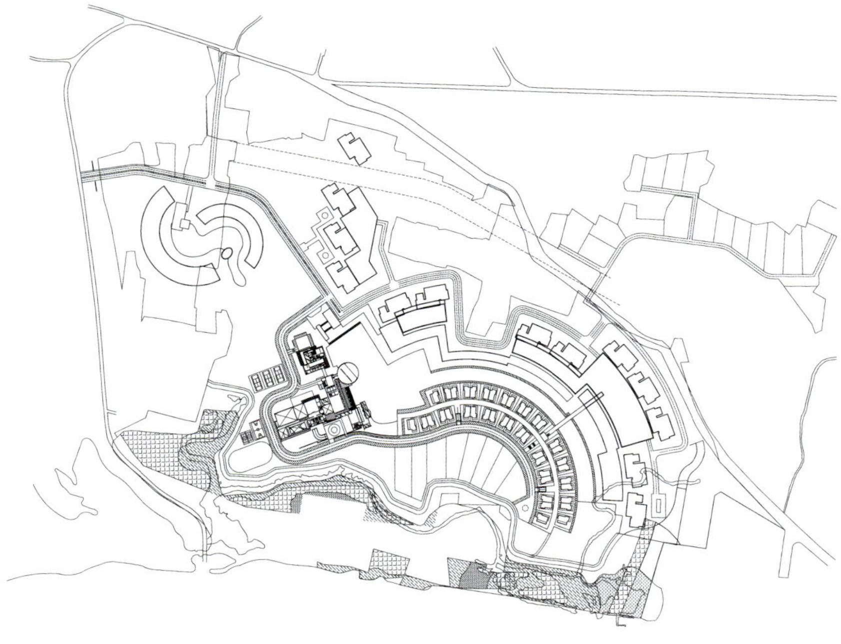

ALIBAUG LODHA

CUSCADEN RESERVE

Singapore, 2018

Situated within the central part of Singapore, a developing residential area close to the Orchard Road commercial belt, Cuscaden Reserve occupies a relatively narrow sloped site, fronting two main roads. A site bounded by high-rise developments, the desire was to create a distinct architectural solution with well-crafted interior and exterior spaces.

The design vision for Cuscaden Reserve was to create a cohesive blend of architecture, landscape, and interiors. Inspired by the Bauhaus movement, known for merging art, craftsmanship, and technology, a series of efficiently planned unit modules were conceived around a central core to allow space flexibility and future adaptability.

The building sits elevated at the highest point of the site, offering optimal views towards Orchard Road and the Singapore Botanic Gardens. A long, gently sloped tree lined driveway creates a sense of entry and prolongs the arrival process, culminating in a generous arrival court directly leading to the tower lobbies. The tower footprint was elevated 12 meters above the ground plane allowing the overlap of exterior landscaping with interior space and creating tall volumetric spaces linked to the clubhouse and facilities.

A series of large overlapping terraces at the ground base of the tower create amenity space for the residents while ensuring a sense of privacy from the surroundings. A pavilion clubhouse with alpine green marble feature wall creates a visual axis of entry on arrival, and opens to vistas towards the large mature heritage trees along the site boundary. A grand lawn steps down to a dining pavilion terrace which steps further to the main pool elevated over the adjoining street.

Cuscaden Reserve evokes the essence of tropical urban living through a modern language of design, integrating experiential landscapes with articulated architectural form. A rich interplay of color, materiality, and order, expressed through the architecture, interiors, and landscaping.

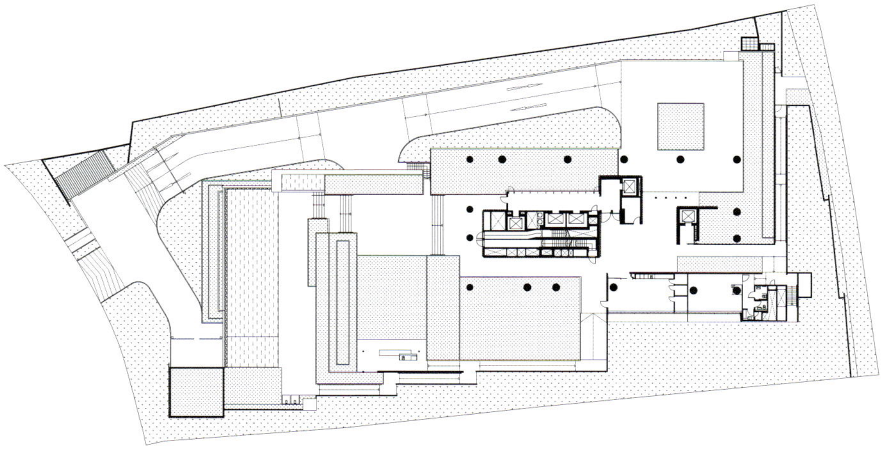

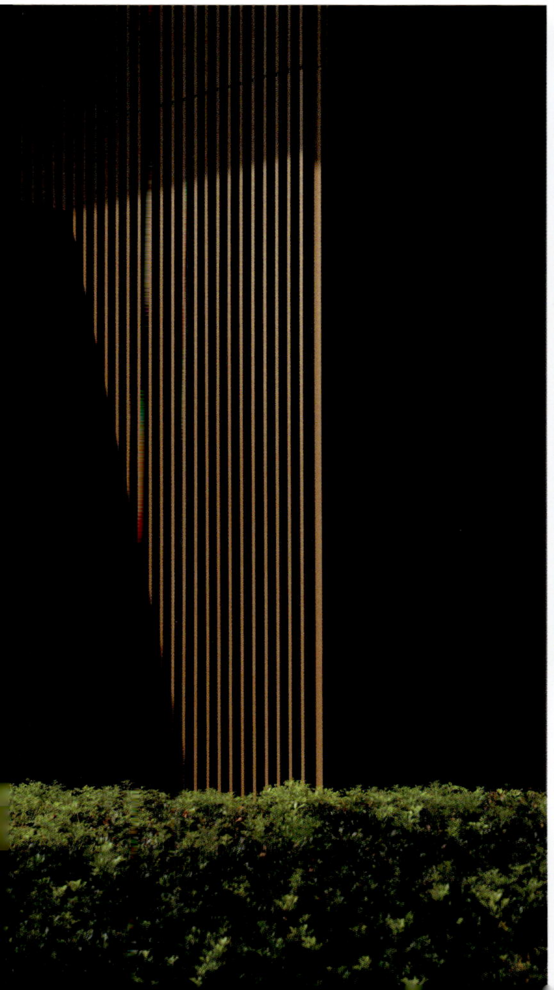

CLUNY PARK RESIDENCE

Singapore, 2011

Positioned sensitively next to the Singapore Botanic Gardens, a UNESCO World Heritage site, Cluny Park Residence offers an unassuming yet defined architectural response to its context. Generous elevated verandahs framed by angled fins provide sun shading, privacy, and a platform for viewing the surrounding gardens and natural landscapes.

The building sits on a long linear site, with its narrower ends facing the prime views to the gardens. Apartment units are lined along a central core with deep balcony spaces provided along its entire length. The balconies are framed by deep timber-clad fins and soffits which align views towards the Singapore Botanic Gardens, while creating privacy from neighboring buildings.

Full-height glass windows blur the boundaries between indoor and outdoor spaces, extending the interiors into the green surroundings. Ground level apartments feature private patios and pools, buffering urban noise through a layering of planting and landscaped features. The upper floors house duplex units with double-height living spaces and high ceilings, enhancing the sense of space and connection with nature.

Communal facilities, including a pool, jacuzzi, barbecue pit, and gym are located on the roof level, providing panoramic views and serving as social hubs for residents and guests. The façade and interior design blend materials and geometries seamlessly. Glazing framed with light composite timber and aluminum sections creates a structured yet organic language. Internally, a lighter color scheme complements warm wood accents, integrating white oak floors, textured brushed-cypress walls, and walnut cabinets. Extruded aluminum trims accentuate the façade's lines, reflecting Cluny Park Residence's modern design ethos, mirroring the serene and verdant environment it inhabits.

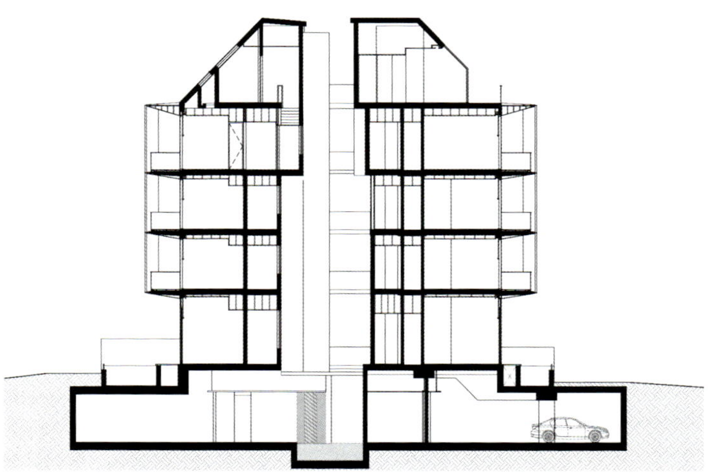

CLUNY PARK
residence

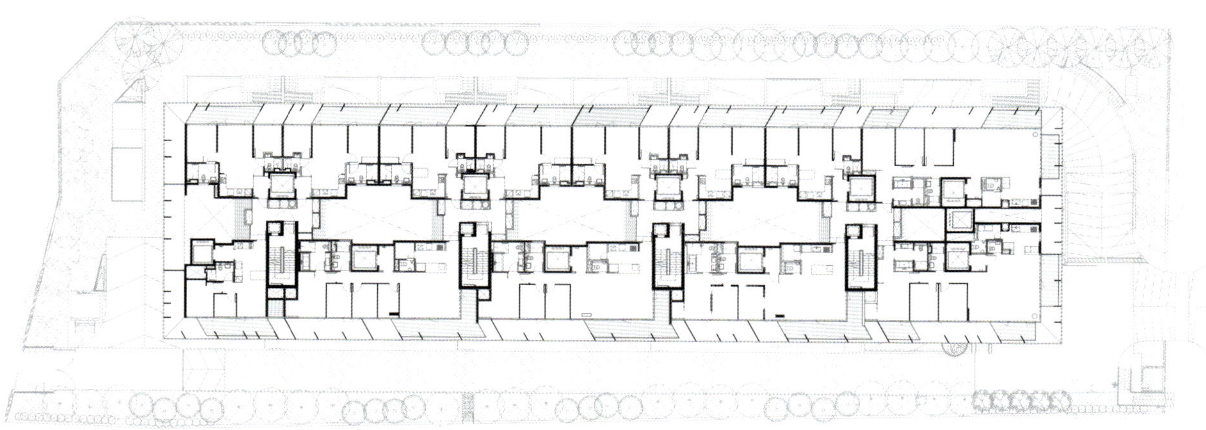

SELETAR PARK RESIDENCES

Singapore, 2011

Seletar Park, set in a landlocked site in a residential neighborhood, was conceived as a perimeter building overlooking a large landscaped courtyard. A unique terracing approach was adopted in order to link the ground-floor and basement, allowing light and ventilation to activate facility spaces on the lower levels, and to create a strong sectional change within an otherwise level site. Alongside the central void, a grand white granite staircase with walls covered in cascading plants descends to the basement floor where the clubhouse's lower level can be accessed. Originating from the infinity pool and bordered by stone planters overflowing with shrubs and creepers, it forms an attractive ensemble to be admired from the balconies.

All residential units are oriented to face inwards into the central garden. Living spaces and bedrooms open up to continuous balconies that line the inner perimeter. Overlapping frames provide further definition and rhythmic articulation to the horizontally dominant expression of these tropical verandahs. The fine edges and sharp lines of these repetitive rectilinear forms break down the continuous massing of the blocks. Internal courtyards are carved out to provide lighting and ventilation to the service areas of the residential units.

From the main arrival, framed by existing rain trees, a walkway lined by reflecting pools and layered greenery leads the visitors towards the central area, where a series of cascades creates a striking water feature. The linear reflecting pools provide a degree of separation and privacy for the garden patios of the ground level units. The integration of architecture and landscape forms a cohesive inward-looking garden environment.

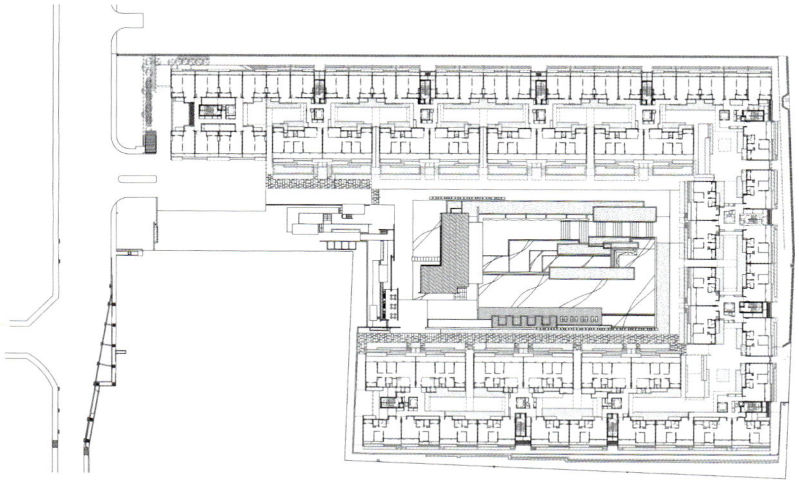

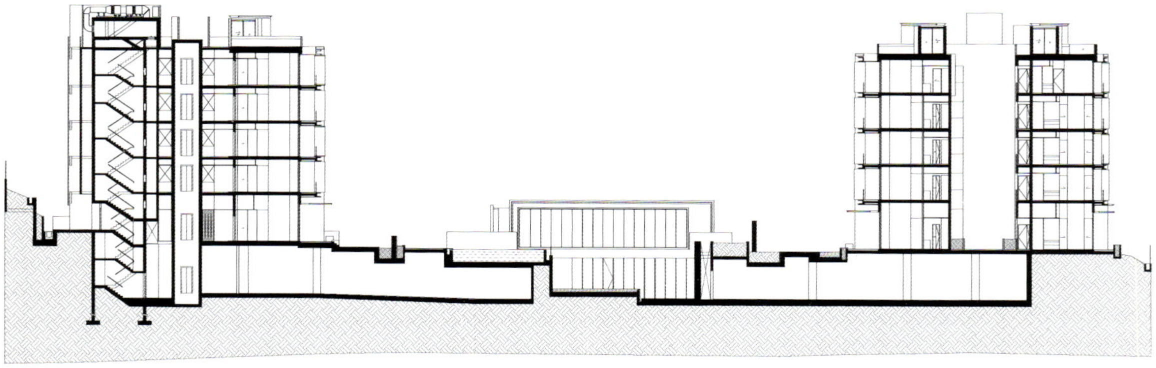

Low Density Developments

Chinese Chamber of Commerce
Founders' Memorial
National Design Centre
Singapore Art Museum
Henbon One Dong'an Gallery
Cuscaden Reserve Gallery
19 Nassim Gallery
Soori Peninsula
Soori Wyoming
Soori Niseko
Maadheli Resort
Riviera Bali
Vanke OCT Nanchang
Kuala Lumpur House
New Delhi House
Tenda

新加坡中華總商會
Singapore Chinese Chamber of Commerce & Industry
CITY HALL SQUARE
OUT
Raised
Zebra
Crossing
GIVE
WAY

CHINESE CHAMBER OF COMMERCE

Singapore, 2016

Established in 1906, the Singapore Chinese Chamber of Commerce and Industry (SCCCI) stands as an emblem of the Chinese business community in Singapore. The recent architectural rejuvenation by SCDA sought to harmonize its rich heritage with a contemporary design approach. The redesign introduces a new rear block, with a concave fritted glass façade, offering a modern architectural narrative in contrast to the conserved historic front façade.

Stepping inside, the SCCCI building's grand lobby tells a story of innovative design and cultural symbolism. The renovation allows the updated lobby to be expanded vertically and horizontally by removing existing columns and employing structural transfers to create a spacious and seamless area for visitors.

Inspired by *feng shui* principles, the lobby design symbolizes prosperity for Singapore's business community. The lobby ceiling draws inspiration from ancient Chinese gold tael coins, symbolizing wealth and prosperity. This symbolic narrative is translated into the ceiling design, where a series of concentric circles emanate from the core, portraying a semblance of the historic coin. The strategic deployment of lighting fixtures crafts a warm and inviting ambiance while carefully chosen materials resonate with the building's historic elegance. The lobby's specific design, lighting, and materials pay tribute to cultural symbolism, reflecting SCCCI's legacy.

The top floor of the existing structure has been extensively remodeled to house the organization's council chamber. Adjacent to this space, sits the new members' lounge, a celebrated space beneath the ornate conserved temple roof and surrounded by roof gardens.

The blend of contemporary elements, illustrated in the undulating glass façade of the new wing, with the historically reverent lobby, captures the essence of SCCCI's heritage in Singapore's contemporary business and cultural landscape.

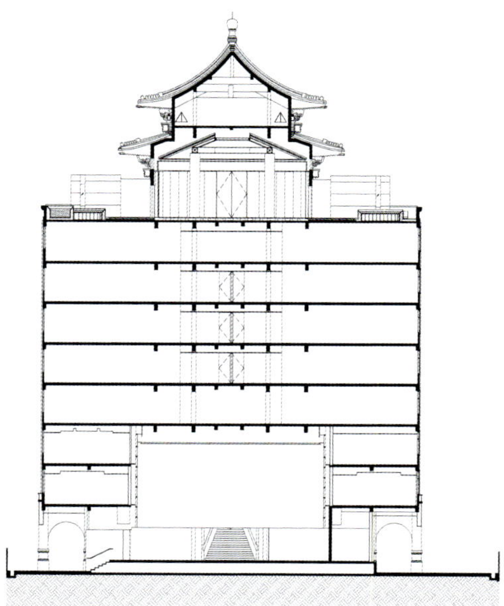

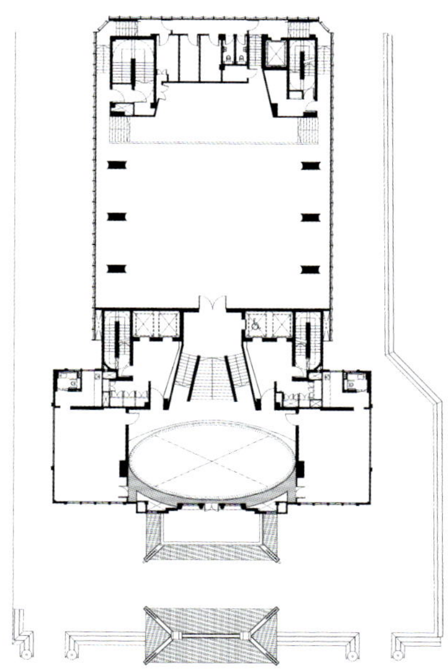

"A multiracial society founded on the concepts of democracy, social equality and socialist concepts of economic and social justice is the only safe and practical way of building a united nation…."
S. Rajaratnam, Deputy Prime Minister 1980 - 85
" We pursued that
me tell you the sky
adventure. And
I say, look at that
Lee Kuan Yew,

FOUNDERS' MEMORIAL

Singapore, 2019

Amidst Singapore's urbanized skyline, the Rain Tree stands as a strong emotional, cultural, and architectural statement, echoing the visionary principles of the Founding Fathers.

Beyond just a sculptural statement, it serves as a contemplative space designed to blend retrospective contemplation with forward-looking inspiration and vision. The design, inspired by the innate character of a sheltering rain tree, a particular species prevalent along the streets and within the green parks of the nation, finds itself grounded in the earth yet aspiring towards the sky.

The Rain Tree sits as a monolith of glass, steel, and stone, an object in space. Within lies a spatial narrative, progressing from underground and reaching to ground level. Starting in the basement, this immersive gallery space delves into Singapore's foundational origins, resonating with historical significance.

Surrounded by an elemental elliptical void, a striking shaft of light acts as a guiding beacon, inviting visitors to ascend towards the oculus. The fluid movement as visitors ascend the ramp surrounding the central void symbolizes progression, a journey towards vitality and growth, mirroring Singapore's own journey of resilience, progress, and transformation.

The culmination of this symbolic journey is the viewing gallery above. The Rain Tree's expansive canopy offers visitors a panoramic view of Singapore's skyline. This elevated vantage point serves as a reminder of the rewards of navigating a remarkable journey.

The Rain Tree, with its purposeful design, embodies not only a physical structure but a story: an architectural testament to Singapore's historical legacy, contemporary identity, and a vision of the future.

"A multiracial society founded on the concepts of democracy, social equality and socialist concepts of economic and social justice is the only safe and practical way of building a united nation...."
S. Rajaratnam, Deputy Prime Minister 1980 - 85
" We pursued that rainbow and that was how we came to build today's Singapore. For the young, let me tell you the sky has turned brighter. There's a glorious rainbow that beckons those with the spirit of adventure. And there are rich findings at the end of the rainbow. To the young and to the not so old, I say, look at that horizon, follow that rainbow, go ride it."
Lee Kuan Yew, Prime Minister 1959 – 90

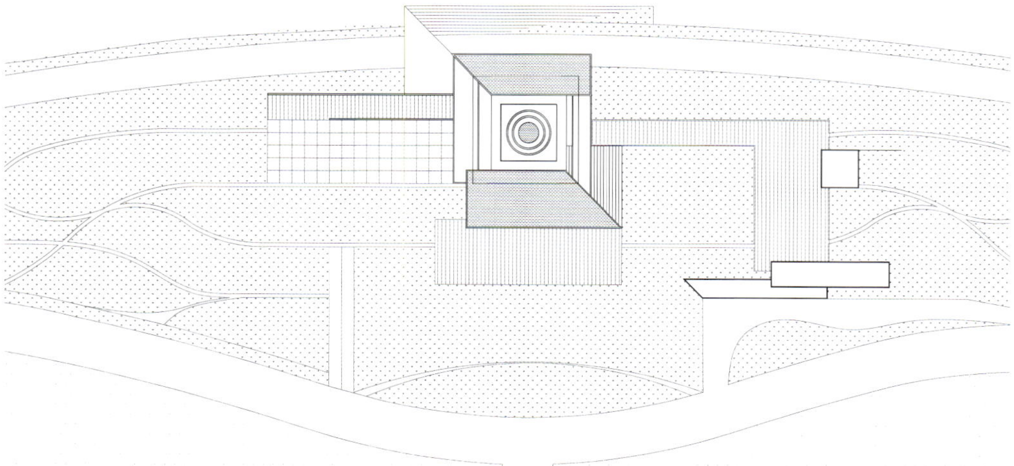

NATIONAL DESIGN CENTRE

Singapore, 2011

The National Design Centre showcases an innovative approach to revitalizing the urban landscape, particularly within the Bras Basah art and conservation district. The project aims to repurpose an existing structure, creating a versatile space for interaction and education.

The design introduces a composition of four translucent boxes, purposefully arranged and overlapping to form interconnected spaces for various public and private uses. These boxes open up internally to a central atrium, inviting the public to engage with the space and activating the central courtyard.

Respecting the existing building, the design insertion enhances the internal spaces while preserving the original structure. The addition of adaptable elements along the Victoria Street façade increases internal volume and transforms previously enclosed areas. These translucent boxes become prominent features within the central courtyard, providing space for displays and exhibitions. Positioned separately from the existing façade, they create three-story light walls that filter natural light into the gallery spaces. Externally, these new volumes complement the conserved façade, blending visually with the surrounding streetscape.

The design also prioritizes activating the street frontage with key public facilities situated on the ground level. A bistro café connects the street to the central courtyard, leading into retail and exhibition spaces. Galleries extend along the central courtyard and continue towards the open court, with additional seating available in an alfresco café area.

The project culminates in an open landscaped terrace on the existing flat roof, providing a quiet space for contemplation and discussion. Illuminated subtly at night, the rooftop and translucent boxes create a dynamic composition of solids and voids, contributing to the vibrancy of the arts precinct.

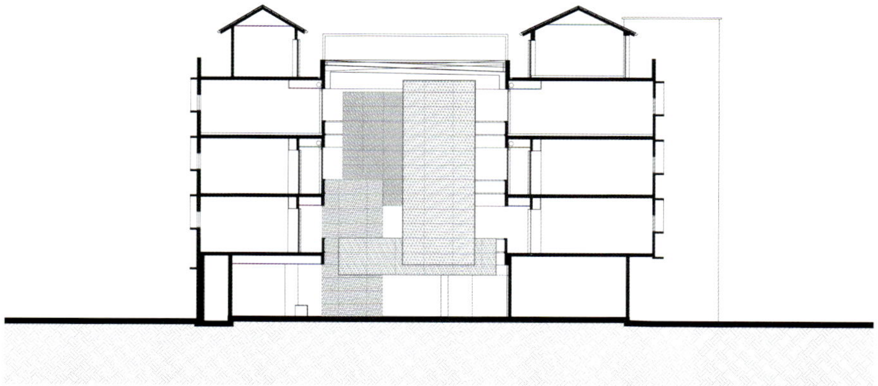

NATIONAL
DESIGN
CENTRE
111 MIDDLE ROAD

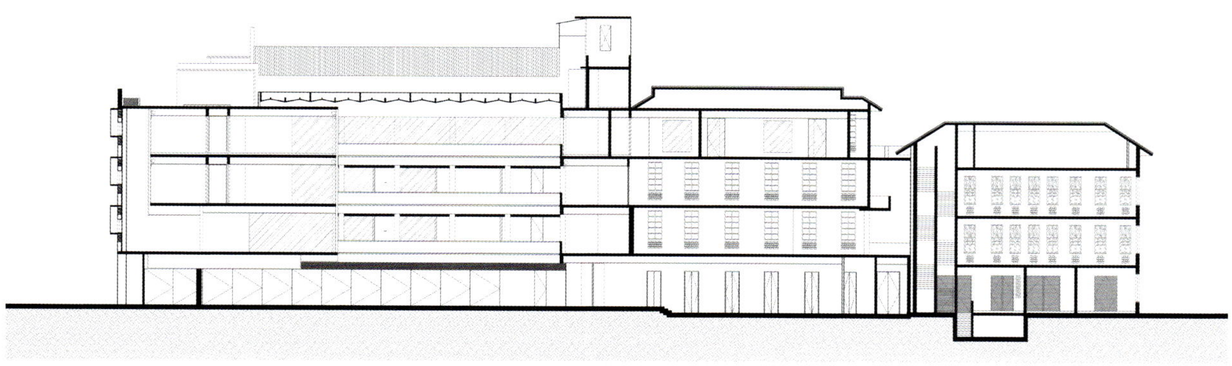

NATIONAL DESIGN CENTRE

singaporeartmuseum

SINGAPORE ART MUSEUM

Singapore, 2018

Provenance for the redesign of the Singapore Art Museum was shaped by the museum's need for more exhibition space to house contemporary art. The response was to float a large enclosed volume above the existing courtyard of the former St. Joseph's Institution. A large column-free exhibition space could then be housed within this box, liberating the historical school building from the stresses of displaying large artwork.

Directly below this suspended volume, the former outdoor courtyard that was the center of the building cluster was now transformed into a spacious, light-filled indoor event area through the use of an innovative suspended glass façade.

The exterior façade of the new floating volume features a series of reflective glass panels running along its length, with each panel progressively angled towards the historical building's dome, creating multiple and displaced reflections of the dome that shift as pedestrians walk past it. The main entrance has been relocated to Queen Street to improve pedestrian access and to create a welcoming outdoor plaza.

This move reemphasizes the historical building's iconic front façade by shifting the vehicular drop-off away and underscores a commitment to prioritizing the visitor experience. The new outdoor plaza at Queen Street also served as a connecting outdoor space to the 8Q annex building further down the road, which was similarly treated with a new volumetric intervention. A connecting bridge between St. Joseph's Institution and the 8Q annex building was also envisioned to finally link the two formerly isolated properties of the art museum.

Overall, the renovation aimed to engage modernity while at the same time actively engaging the past, forming a comprehensive and thoughtful approach to urban evolution in architecture.

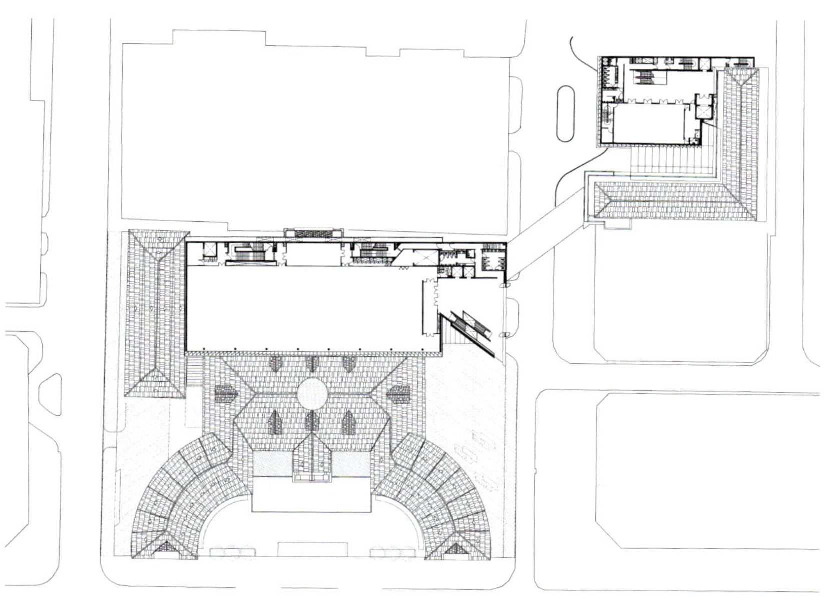

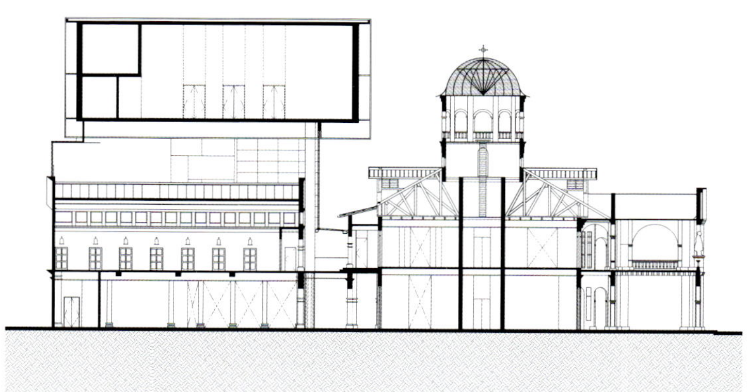

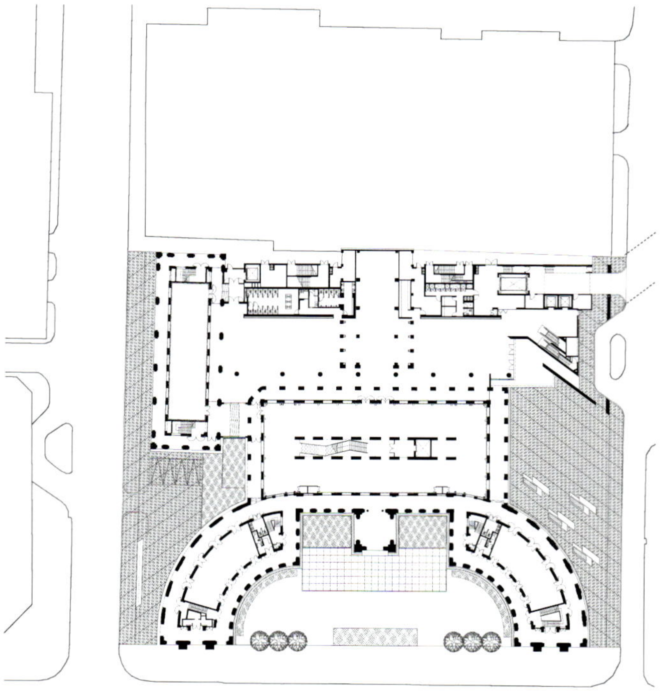

singapore

sam
museum

HENBON ONE DONG'AN GALLERY

Chengdu, China, 2019

Located amidst lush wetland greenery and by Dong'An Lake in the suburbs of Chengdu, One Dong'An mixed-use development presents a design approach that responds directly to its natural surroundings. The One Dong'An Gallery, situated within the larger development, serves both as a sales center and residents' club, offers a glimpse of this approach, providing uninterrupted views of the surrounding eco-park and Long Quan Mountain.

The gallery stands as an architectural statement, celebrating defined geometries of line, texture, and volume. Stacked glass boxes form expressive overhangs and precise edges, accented by champagne metal mesh façades that glow softly at night. A stepped-bottom reflecting pool serves as a focal point, echoing the gallery's angular reflected form, defined by geometric landscaped feature walls, a wraparound outdoor deck and sharply manicured hedges. Interiorly, the space contrasts an enclosed ground floor with a fully glazed upper story, offering a flood of natural light and glimpses of the surrounding eco-park.

Feature walls with tactile, textured surfaces highlight sculptural elements, serving as a backdrop for sales models and visual information of the development. A central feature staircase, sculptural in form, anchors the interior spaces as a strong vertical element, connecting the major spaces of the gallery with the quieter and more private functions below. The basement houses a private club with residents' lounge, tea and private dining rooms, anchored by a top-lit pool, bringing dramatic reflected light into the space.

The project emphasizes natural material with clearly defined details, reflecting a commitment to architectural form and structural coherence.

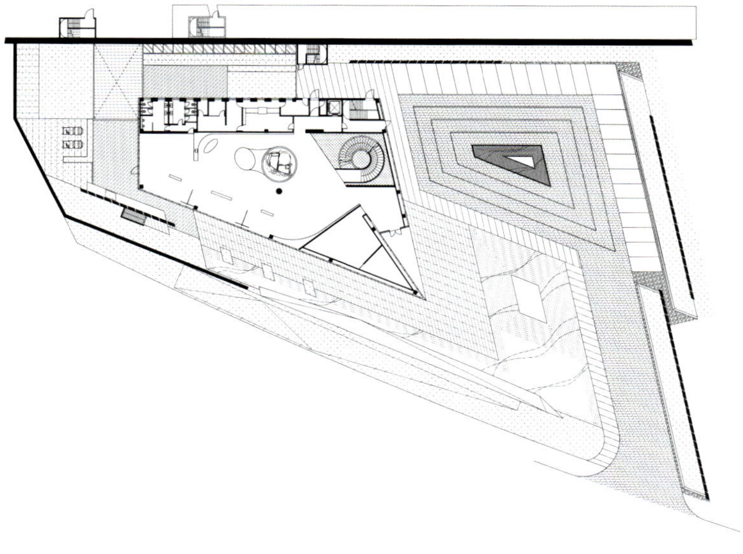

CUSCADEN
RESERVE

CUSCADEN RESERVE GALLERY

Singapore, 2018

The project was commissioned as a temporary gallery and show unit space for the future Cuscaden Reserve residential project, situated on the same location within the site along Cuscaden Road.

A large steel-structured glass pavilion sits elevated above the street level, cantilevered over lush green planting. The structure of the pavilion is expressed and celebrated on the exterior of the pavilion, allowing the internal spaces to be uncluttered and column-free. The box serves as the main gallery space, showcasing the project model and visual representations of the development. A central organizing wall clad in Verde Alpi marble forms a structural axis for the building and hides the administrative areas behind. The ceiling soffit, consisting of large gridded translucent panels, glows gently as light fades, giving a distinctive sculptural quality to the form. The gallery and show flat unit are placed around a stepped central arrival courtyard, with a glazed bridge link fronting a large reflective water body and sculpture. The journey through the sales gallery is choreographed to control views within the landscape spaces and obscure views to larger surrounding buildings. The show unit opens visually to a quiet Caesalpinia tree lawn, with light filtering into the interior space through a series of deep vertical façade fins.

A bold, yet quiet and contemplative space, the gallery strives for simplicity in its architectural form, focusing on the resolution of detail, balanced materiality, and a sequential flow of space from its interior to exterior.

CUSCADEN RESERVE GALLERY

19 NASSIM GALLERY

Singapore, 2019

Through the integration of frame and form, light and shadow, the 19 Nassim Gallery employs traditional modernist ideals while offering a fresh design language representative of the development's ethos.

In concept, the gallery consists of three main components: form, frame, and landscape.

A clear structural frame interlocks with a monolithic travertine volume, creating visual tension and contrast. This interlocking frame implies a volume of space, seemingly floating above the adjacent garden and inviting visitors to enter. By composing these architectural relationships, the gallery cultivates a sense of place, serenity, and simplicity.

At the edges of the gallery, a linear reflecting pool further defines the design language. The combination of water and landscape creates an interplay of rippling light and shadow, softening the transition and procession between exterior and interior. Entering the gallery, visitors are welcomed by a simple space anchored by a single screen which separates the public and private functions of the building. Within this main space, the 19 Nassim development is presented by an articulate architectural model, curated materials, furniture, and lighting. The two main volumes of the gallery are arranged in response to the site geometries to surround an inner garden court, a central light-filled organizing space connecting the architectural ensemble, punctuated by a single sculptural tree sitting in a field of river pebbles.

The 19 Nassim Gallery tells the story of the broader development through a clear modernist approach, offering archetypal forms and curated spatial relationships. Materials are kept intentionally simple and understated to complement the minimal formal expression of the architectural volumes and to allow the displays to be experientially celebrated.

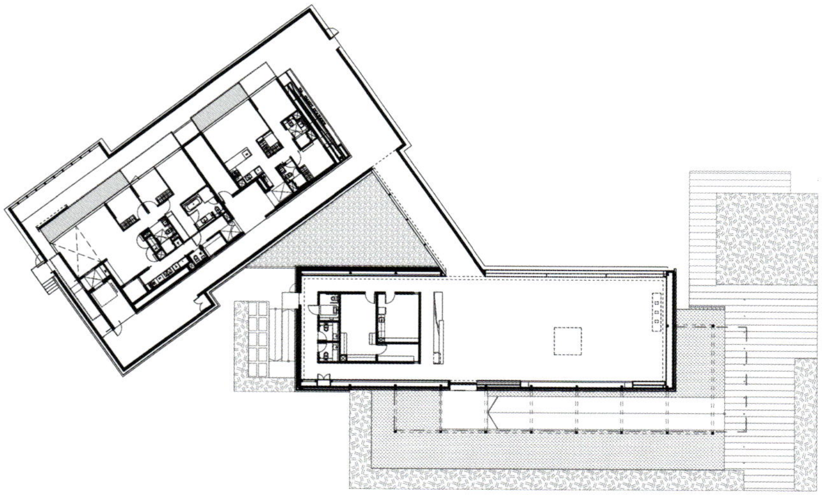

SOORI PENINSULA

Bali, Indonesia, 2025

Keiyo is located within Soori Bali, a serene coastal retreat in the Tabanan regency of Bali—an area celebrated for its breath-taking natural beauty and rich agricultural heritage. Perched on a dramatic cliff edge, the restaurant offers uninterrupted views of the Indian Ocean and black sand beach, surrounded by vibrant paddy fields and nestled beside a sacred Balinese temple that has stood for over 70 years.

Housed in a glass-enclosed, thatch-roofed pavilion that echoes the form of a traditional Balinese bale (or traditional Balinese pavilion), the restaurant seamlessly blends ancient design with modern elegance. To the west, the imposing peak of Mount Batukaru looms in the distance, anchoring the landscape in spiritual and geological significance.

Construction of the restaurant uses time-honored Balinese materials that root the space in its natural and cultural surroundings. Its soaring roof is a traditional Balinese thatch roof, providing both texture and a sense of timeless craftsmanship. Teak wood, prized for its strength and rich patina, forms the pavilion's elegant structural frame, while the foundation is built from locally sourced volcanic stone—anchoring the restaurant to the very cliffs that overlook the Indian Ocean. Together, these materials evoke a deep connection to Bali's architectural traditions and elemental landscape.

SOORI WYOMING

Wyoming, USA, 2020

Soori Wyoming is envisioned as an ecological retreat, created to inspire and empower travelers in the exploration of new ways of creating, thinking, and living. The retreat takes shape as a herd of self-sustaining cabins, a provocation of how architecture and design can rally to make palatable off-grid hospitality a real proposition.

In homage to the sense of community and inspired by settlements in the area which congregated along the fertile banks of rivers, the cabins are configured across a plateau in linear fashion, creating a main street or communal thoroughfare while ensuring sweeping views of the surroundings for each cabin. The necklace of cabins culminates in a main house that serves as a reception, gathering space, and point of reference. Surrounding the retreat are acres of national land, with Bald Ridge and the Beartooth Mountains serving as a dramatic backdrop to the Clarks Fork Yellowstone River.

Designed to physically and visually blend with its natural surroundings through the use of concrete mixed with natural pigments and stone aggregate from its surroundings, the resort hugs the slope and assumes a low profile within its context, respecting the existing topography while incorporating some of the larger rock outcroppings and native flora into the design.

Gravel roads and pedestrian pathways minimize visual impact on the surroundings, while recreating the tactile experience of hiking through the moraine landscape. Large windows and openings in the architecture will admit a generous amount of daylight into the resort interior, minimizing the need for artificial light. With objectives firmly set towards carbon neutrality, the resort will be primarily powered by solar energy fed from a nearby on-site solar array and will utilize electrical or induction appliances in its kitchens, and electrical heating that avoids the use of fossil fuels.

Soori Wyoming's vision is holistic and reaches beyond design. It represents an attitude towards community-building, in harmony with nature. Just as we hold each other accountable in mankind's quest for sustainability, the architecture of each cabin proves just as important as their assemblage: creating a shared, nurturing communal space.

SOORI NISEKO

Niseko, Japan, 2021

Soori Niseko seeks to capture the essence and spirit of Niseko, an expanding village in Hokkaido, well known as a popular destination for skiing during the winter months. The site sits perched on the gentle slopes of Upper Hirafu, with spectacular views of the surrounding slopes and further towards the famous Mount Yotei.

Conceived as a low-scale, sensitively curated resort, the building steps gently towards the ski slopes, responding to the site topography while creating a series of outdoor terraces with views over the low-rise village. The ground and lower floor zones are curated to respond to the lifestyles of the guests. A central lobby with a warming fireplace connects to a ski-in/ski-out lounge with lockers, while a small bistro café sits at the edge of the site with access to an outdoor terrace.

Utilizing a palette of dark metal, wood, and warm orange terracotta, the façade materiality echoes the feel of a warm traditional hideaway, a space to retreat from the elements. Vertical slot windows are positioned to capture the best views and are balanced with solid wall panels to reduce the reflective impact of the building. The interior of each unit has been designed to maximize flexibility for different user groups, with adaptable spaces converted as needed. The interior design embodies the craft and attention to details traditionally found in Japanese interiors, while installing a modern, progressive approach. The rigorous simplicity of the space, combined with the light timber palette and clean lines, allows for one's focus to be led to the outstanding surrounding views.

Soori Niseko endeavors to add a sensitive built form to the constantly expanding streetscape. Through a careful balance of warm materiality and clean architectural lines, it sits respectfully within its site, embracing the uniqueness and spirit of the surrounding context.

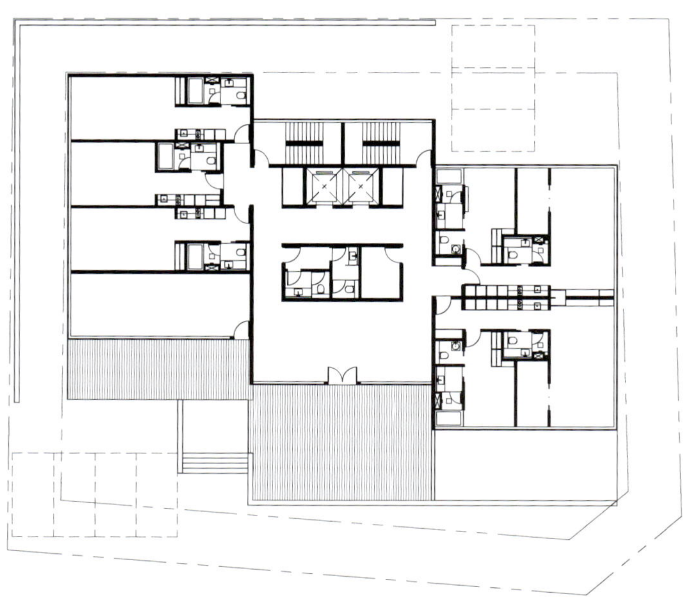

MAADHELI RESORT

Maldives, 2024

Envisioned as a luxury resort in the Maldives, this 87-key resort sits on a natural island surrounded by a large expansive sheltered lagoon. The existing main island features 23 hectares of coconut groves, natural sandy beaches, and a rocky beach to its south. From the beginning of the project, concerted effort was taken to identify the island's natural features and design the resort to be sensitively integrated.

Conceived as a curation of archipelagos, small clusters of private villas that sit directly over the water. Each cluster of 11 villas is connected by a meandering boardwalk that flows through green space and opens to expansive views out over the ocean. Each water villa benefits from a backdrop of lush greenery that frames the azure waters of the Maldivian sea.

Along the coastline, natural island beach villas are discreetly nestled within the existing vegetation, imbuing guests with the sensation that they are residing in an ecologically sensitive dwelling that is an integral part of the island. The central public facilities to the north of the main island are a collection of discreet low-scale pavilions, designed around a central event space which faces the deepest natural beach on the island. This allows for a high degree of interaction between the different guest facilities, while being presented with dramatic unobstructed sunset views.

Much of the natural vegetation is planned to be retained, with each villa position carefully marked out to maintain key areas of tree growth. The rocky beaches to the south are treated as a feature, which resulted in the deliberate design interaction of key public facilities with these beaches. Guest experience is not limited to the beaches alone, but also within the depth of the island which features soaring coconut trees.

The architecture of the villas is intentionally kept simple with a focus on form and careful detailing. Deep overhanging geometric roofs are kept low at their eaves to protect against the harsh tropical sunlight and driving rain. The roof volume expresses itself internally to create high internal ceilings through each room where their structure is expressed. The floating villa roofs are lit gently at night, creating a series of abstract forms within the abundance of landscape.

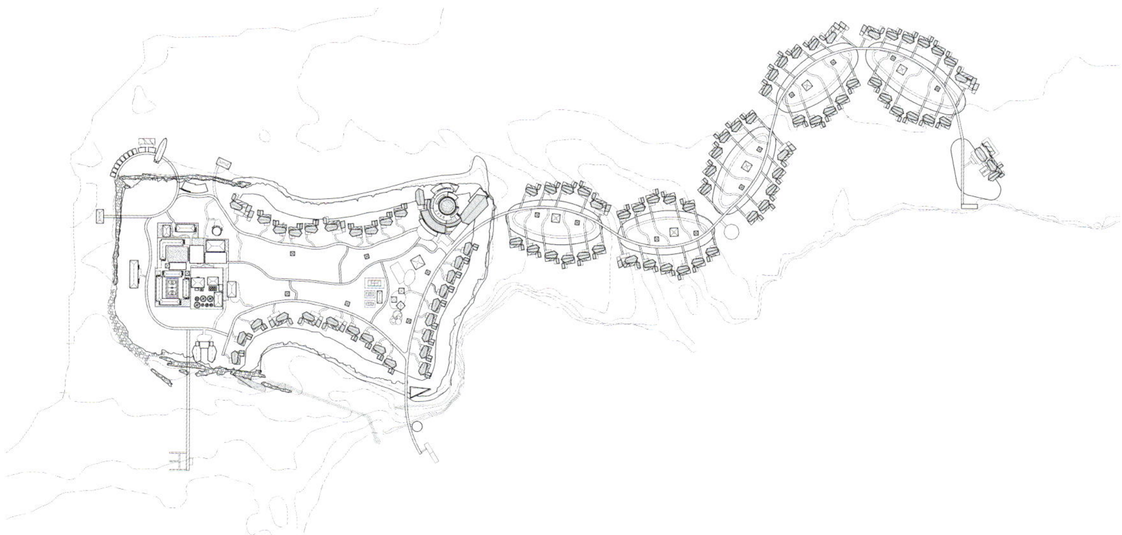

MAADHELI RESORT

RIVIERA BALI

Bali, Indonesia, 2023

Riviera Bali is a residential resort situated on Kura Kura, a 498-hectare island, 15 minutes east of Ngurah Rai International Airport. The master planning takes precedence from an existing waterway connector that runs down the center of the site. The waterway becomes a catalyst and an opportunity to create a unique approach to circulation and landscaping.

The master plan accommodates 179 villas arranged in linear clusters interconnected to a large central canal planned to connect to the future marina.

The mix of 2.5 story villas and residences are strung along small waterway canals lined with tropical landscaping that branch off the main canal, creating a water pathway to each villa. Landscaped promenades meander along the canal edge linking the development to the surrounding future development. Lush landscaping steps gently through each space with a rich Balinese tropical landscape by the water.

The residences which are a combination of bungalows, semi-detached dwellings, and town houses, utilize sectional changes to create privacy and to gently step down to the linear waterways.

Both contemporary and tropical in language, the villas are composed of monolithic pitched forms, clad in terracotta and natural stone. A layer of decorative screens provide shade to external balcony spaces and terraces, laser cut in overlapping metal geometries, the screen provides a crafted element to the clean architectural language.

A larger clubhouse sits at the southern bend of the canal, a prominent focal point in the master plan. A series of folding roof shades shelter indoor and outdoor spaces such as a lounge, restaurant, spa with fitness center, and flexible function rooms. The clubhouse, gently folding along the river's edge, creates a distinctive landmark that fits within the human scale of the development.

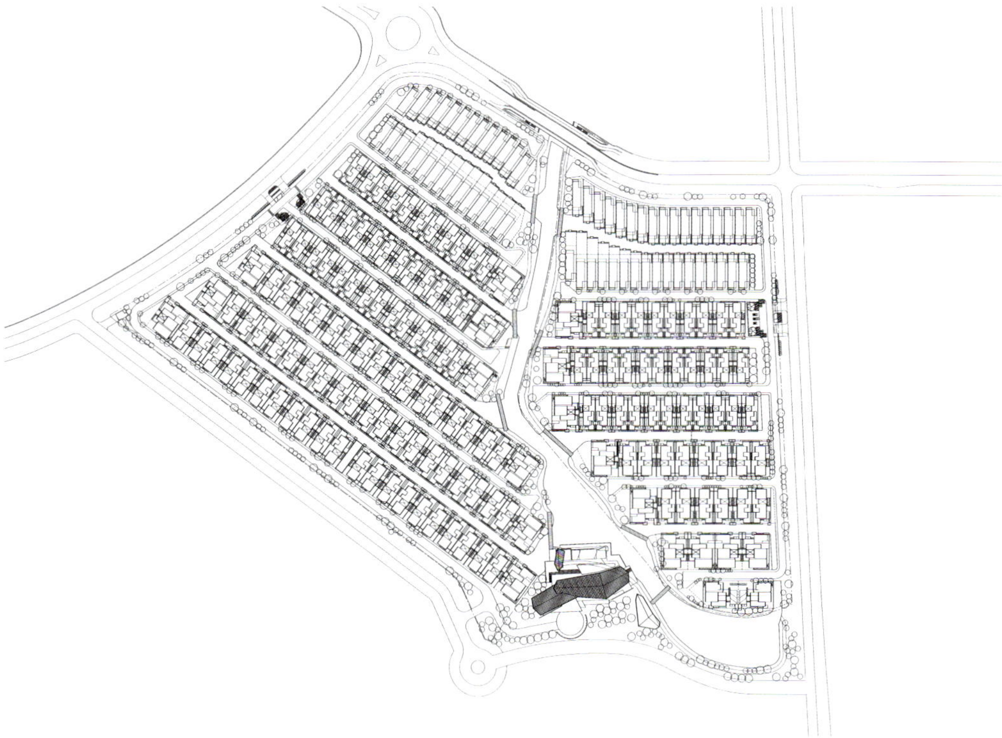

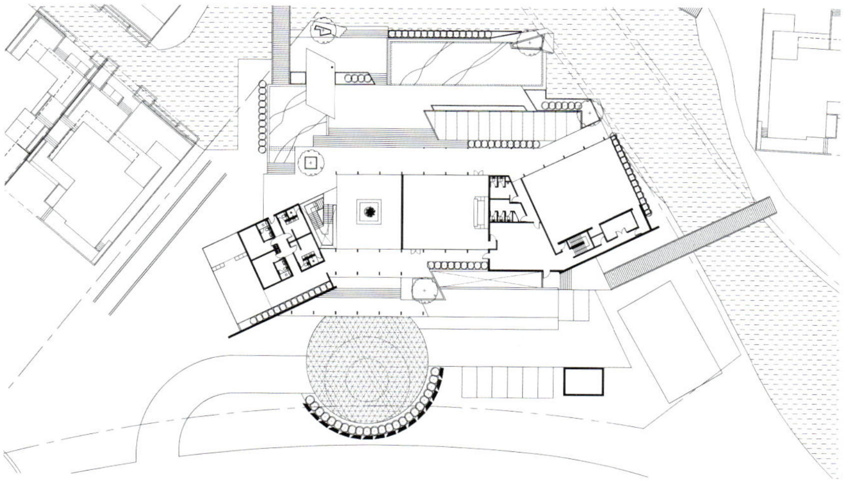

VANKE OCT NANCHANG

Nanchang, China, 2019

Adjacent to XiangHu Wetland Park in Nanchang, SCDA's residential project is a departure from China's standardized urban environments, offering a design inspired by traditional village typologies, while embracing the nuances of traditional Chinese architecture.

In formulating the master plan, emphasis was placed on controlling and differentiating the scale and proportion of the spaces between the clusters, as well as the various avenues and smaller pathways leading to the villas.

The entrance along Qiaoxiang Road leads to an intimate drop-off court. Seven clusters of villas are connected by wide landscaped avenues. Each cluster has its own entry gate, providing a sense of privacy. Residents access their homes through shared courtyards and narrow lanes within each cluster.

The refined architectural language emphasizes simplicity and austerity across the 73 villas. Integrated façade and roofs in modules of two or three villas create a cohesive composition. The minimalist architecture provides a canvas for the landscape design, allowing greenery to play a prominent role.

In consideration of the temperate climate, the north and south façade are treated differently. Main spaces and windows are concentrated on the sunnier south side, while the north side features solid walls, addressing privacy concerns between adjacent villas.

The south façade incorporates metal louvers on window frames, adding detail to the minimalist expression. Sculpturally treated north façade integrates stone screens with protruding gable walls, creating a timeless and rhythmic design.

Material selection reinforces the modern aesthetic, with large-format white aluminum panels for the villa façade and champagne aluminum profiles detailing the windows. The combination of white porcelain-like surfaces and metallic window details accentuates a clean and contemporary expression. The first-floor courtyard walls showcase richly textured granite, establishing a vivid contrast between lower and upper volumes, reinforcing the architectural design concept.

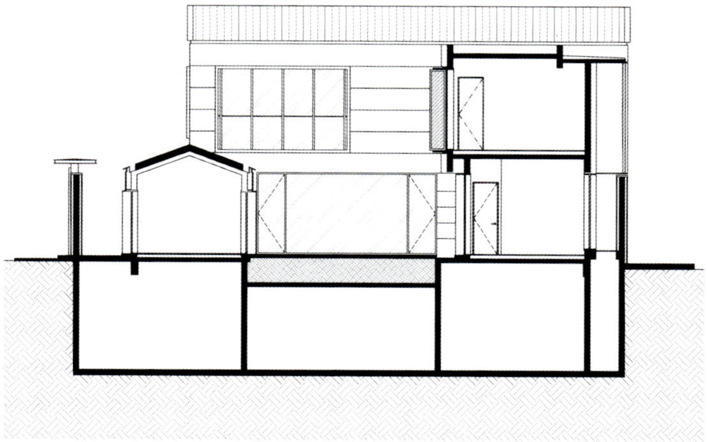

KUALA LUMPUR HOUSE

Kuala Lumpur, Malaysia, 2011

Kuala Lumpur (KL) House offers an escape from the surrounding urbanity where the design weaves together landscape, architecture, and interiors crafted to suit the environment and climate. Drawing inspiration from classical architectural principles, each aspect of KL House explores procession, volume, line, and plane to produce a composed living space.

A series of planned courtyards are positioned in a careful sequence, creating order to the building layout and curating views to each space, with the focus leading to a large central lawn connected to the main living spaces. This outdoor lawn and garden deck wraps around a swimming pool, which forms the nucleus of the architectural composition together with the indoor living rooms.

The building's elevated position allows for the maximization of privacy through sectional interplay, creating open unfolding terrace and garden spaces and semi-submerged private courtyards.

The façade uses a base palette of light champagne aluminum cladding, with window and door cut-outs expressed by sloped soffits clad in timber strips. Each material change is highlighted by thin graphite aluminum edging to create lightness and sharpness to the built form. A light pale stone wall in varying texture runs through the exterior of the house, contributing to the simplicity of the façade expression from forming an arrival courtyard to defining and creating warmth to the semi-indoor spaces.

By utilizing a clear spatial diagram to organize the plan, the house becomes an efficient composition that is free to maximize the integration of outdoor space and generous landscaping to create a holistic living environment.

KUALA LUMPUR HOUSE

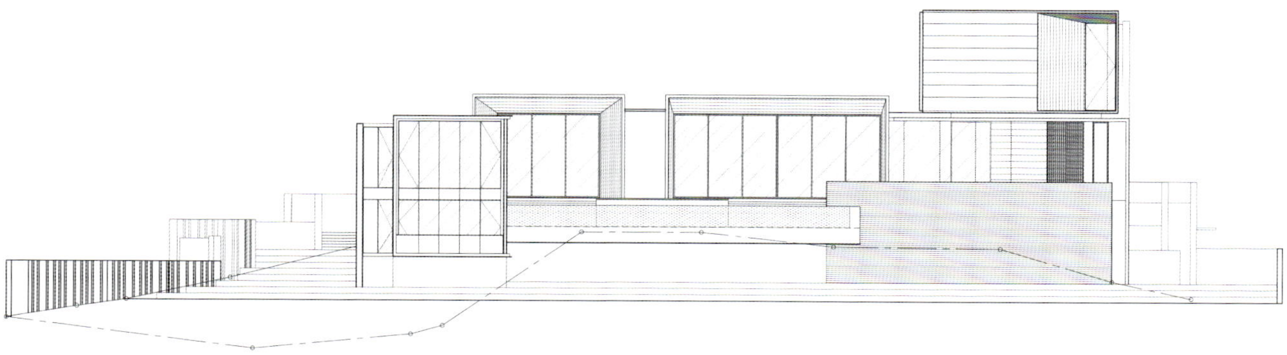

THE LITTLE BLACK JACKET

NEW DELHI HOUSE

New Delhi, India, 2012

Situated within the historic Lutyens' Delhi, this residential complex comprises a family of buildings, the compound strategically arranged around a central sunken water court, a private space for residents and guests.

Taking inspiration from the vernacular haveli town houses of India's western region, the architecture strikes a delicate balance between solid and void, architecture and landscape, through carefully configured spatial relationships, materials, and experiences. The design palette revolves around two key elements: white granite and weathered timber, creating both a diverse yet cohesive architecture. These materials, detailed with variations in finish and pattern, adorn the walls, landscape features, and walkway.

The architectural layout unfolds sequentially, with meandering exterior corridors connecting reflecting pools, lawns, and pavilions seamlessly. Throughout the grounds, there is continued relationship between building and nature with the integration of outdoor spaces spilling into interior functions of the architecture.

The architecture is anchored by a main house with living and dining spaces in direct connection to the formal garden and stepped courtyard beyond. The other wings, comprising informal living spaces, are composed and arranged to form courtyards, both open-sided and enclosed, with existing mature trees conserved and celebrated as primary objects within the landscape.

In essence, this residential complex in Lutyens' Delhi transcends the concept of mere housing; it is a testament to architectural continuity, integrated landscaping, a celebration of formal lawns, and a variety of richly planted gardens. Amidst the serene surroundings, residents are invited to embrace a lifestyle of elegance and timeless sophistication.

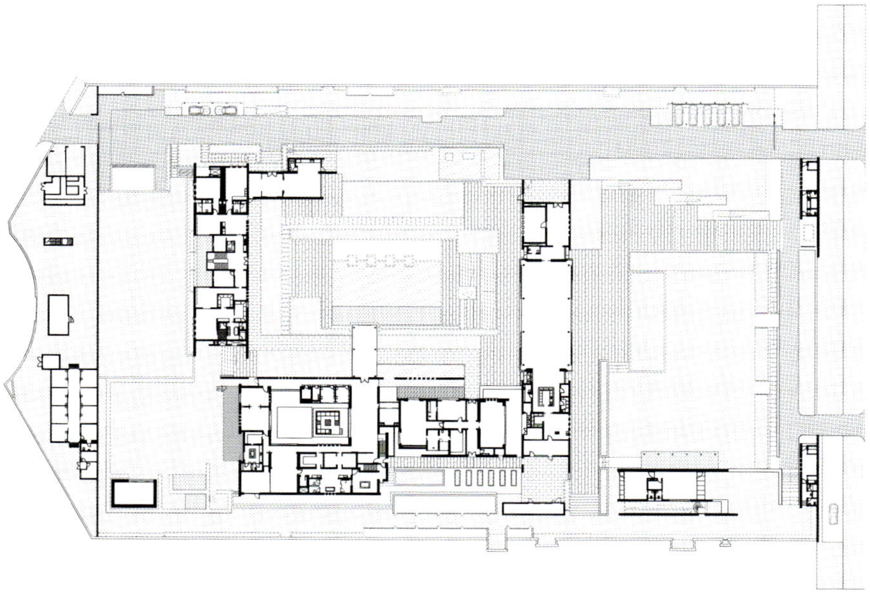

NEW DELHI HOUSE

TENDA

Worldwide, 2020

The Tenda (Bahasa for tent) is an ecologically empathetic retreat created by SCDA to inspire and empower travelers in the exploration of new ways of creating, thinking and living on our finite, green-and-blue planet.

Situated in Kelating village, just minutes from Soo K Chan's Soori Bali, the retreat takes shape as an assembly of self-sustaining cabins, a discursive provocation of how architecture and design can rally to make palatable off-grid living a real proposition.

Conceived as a modular kit of parts designed to be quickly assembled and taken down, each cabin is reminiscent of a deconstructed Dom-Ino House, a locally-inflected Farnsworth House, or a radicalized cabana, depending on who's asking. Unapologetically modernist, each cabin uses several self-sustaining systems that go hand-in-hand with its architecture and is as dependent on nature for its functionality as its constituent parts are dependent on each other.

The solar-paneled roof slides up-and-forward to enclose a serambi-like verandah space, exposing the shower to the sky. At the same time, surface run-off from the roof is kept in a storage tank, filtered, treated and fed back into the cabin for use in the bath, while a water-free, self-composting toilet keeps things hygienic and low-maintenance, says Chan.

Sheathed in slatted screens made from local timber, the simple post-and-beam structure envelops a single bedroom and bath but can be adapted and grouped together to form different configurations.

Designed to be modular, adaptable dwellings with no reliance on infrastructure, the concept that the Tenda posits can just as likely be adapted to other locations, geographies, climates, and experiences.

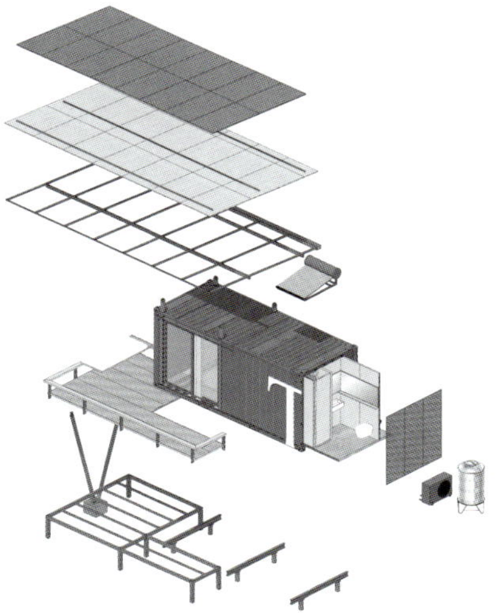

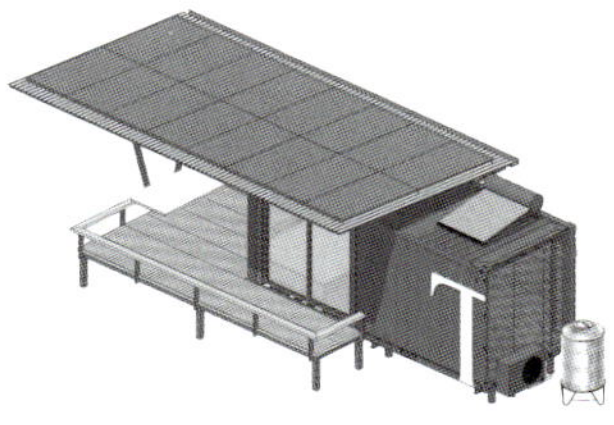

CBU 拳盟中华赛事体验馆

CHRONOLOGY

Dubai Downtown
Dubai, UAE, 2025

The Langham Riyadh
Saudi Arabia, 2023

Yunda Ritz Carlton Changsha
Hunan, China, 2023

Eden Ekkamai
Bangkok, Thailand, 2022

Grand Hyatt Binh Chau
Binh Chau, Vietnam, 2022

HDB Bukit Merah
Singapore, 2022

Peace Centre
Singapore, 2022

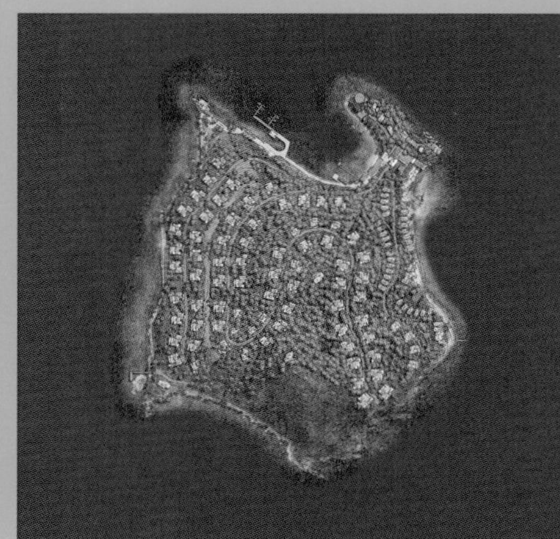

Ritz Carlton Resort
Hon Mot Island, Vietnam, 2022

Suryam Repose by the Water
Ahmedabad, India, 2022

Antiqua Bay Resort
Antigua, Caribbean, 2021

Catskills
New York, USA, 2021

Gemdale Xinsha
Shenzhen, China, 2021

Guofeng Residences
Rizhao, China, 2021

Hyatt Regency Phnom Penh
Phnom Penh, Cambodia, 2021

Red Sea Resort
Saudi Arabia, 2021

St. Regis Liyang
Changzhou, China, 2021

The Australian Centre Weilai
Zhengzhou, China, 2020

Citymark Wuzi
Shenzhen, China, 2020

Fantasia Shenzhen
Shenzhen, China, 2020

Fantasia Wuhan
Wuhan, China, 2020

Four Seasons Vanzhong
Xi’an, China, 2020

Guangda Mixed-use
Dongguan, China, 2020

Haiwei Mixed-use
Hangzhou, China, 2020

Poly Xiancun
Guangzhou, China, 2020

Ritz Carlton Xinliwang
Taichung, Taiwan, 2020

Boracay Resort
Boracay, Philipines, 2019

Henbon One Dong’an
Chengdu, China, 2019

Hyatt Regency Ha Long Bay
Ha Long Bay, Vietnam, 2019

Lanso Jinzhong
Shanxi, China, 2019

Rivière Gallery
Singapore, 2019

Strelka KB
Moscow, Russia, 2019

Unilab Mixed-use
Manila, Philippines, 2019

Weilai Zhengzhou Mixed-use
Zhengzhou, China, 2019

Amber Park Gallery
Singapore, 2018

CDC Daken
Taichung, Taiwan, 2018

The Estelle
Bangkok, Thailand, 2018

Jing Villas
Suzhou, China, 2018

22 Malacca Street
Singapore, 2018

Vanke Dalian
Dalian, China, 2018

Ayala Seda Sicogon
Sicogon Island, Philippines, 2017

Cikande Jakarta
Jakarta, Indonesia, 2017

Kangqiao 200
Zhengzhou, China, 2017

Qianhai Residences
Shenzhen, China, 2017

Royal Mansour Tangiers
Tangiers, Morocco, 2017

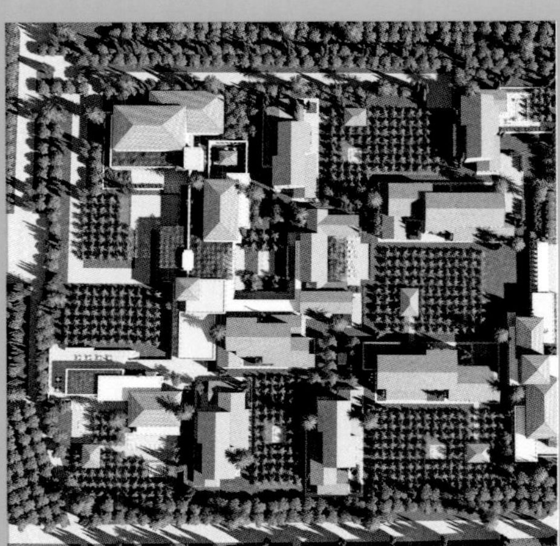

Royal Mansour Rabat
Rabat, Morocco, 2017

Seda Resort Dapdap Mactan
Cebu, Philippines, 2017

Emma Island D
Maldives, 2016

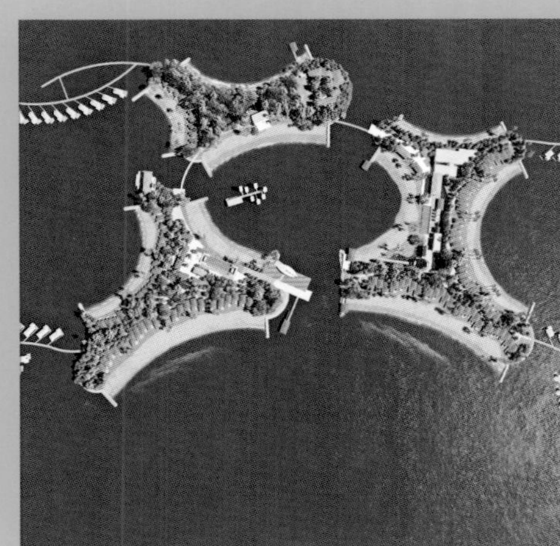

Emma Island FG
Maldives, 2016

Gold Finance
Hangzhou, China, 2016

Guangwu Haikou
Hainan, China, 2016

Ritz Carlton Hongqiao
Shanghai, China, 2016

Ritz Carlton QianDaoHu
Hangzhou, China, 2016

Solis Taihu
Jiangsu, China, 2016

Hindustan Mills
Mumbai, India, 2015

One Central Avenue
Mumbai, India, 2015

519 W 29th
New York, USA, 2015

59th Avenue
New York, USA, 2014

Four Seasons Lijiang
Yunnan, China, 2014

Ginza 2-Chome
Tokyo, Japan, 2014

Park Central Makati
Manila, Philippines, 2014

San Mei Bay Resort
Sanya, China, 2014

Seda Lio Palawan
Palawan, Philippines, 2014

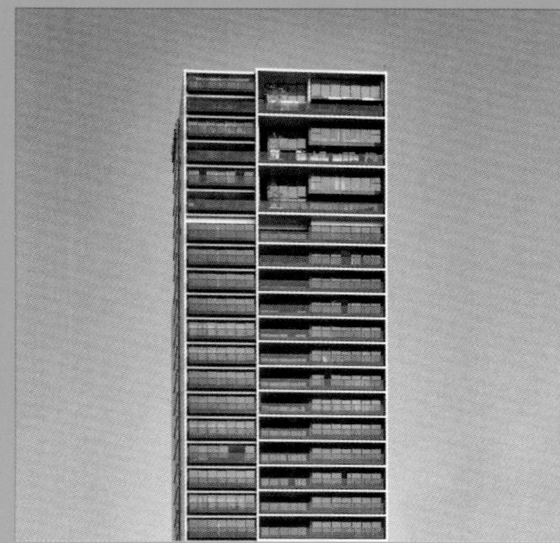

Tela
Bangkok, Thailand, 2014

Anandamaya
Jakarta, Indonesia, 2013

Arzuria
Jakarta, Indonesia, 2013

5th Avenue
New York, USA, 2013

Fiamma Jalan Ampang
Kuala Lumpur, Malaysia, 2013

Waldorf Astoria Haitang Bay
Sanya, China, 2013

Al Muneera
Abu Dhabi, UAE, 2012

Echelon
Singapore, 2012

Casa Domaine
Jakarta, Indonesia, 2011

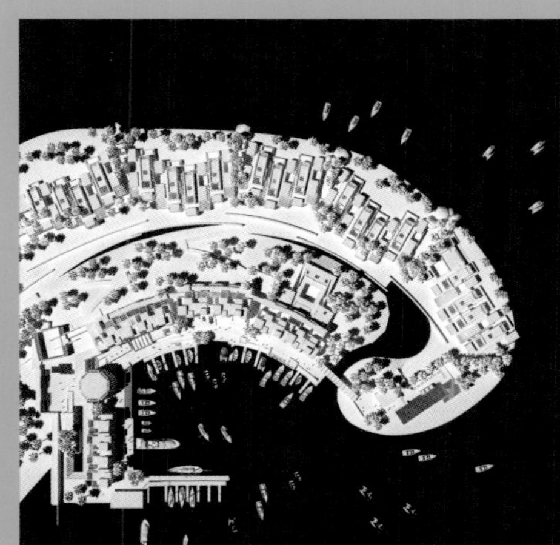

Project Square One
Abu Dhabi, UAE, 2011

Acknowledgments

I will like to take this opportunity to express my appreciation to the numerous individuals and organizations that have supported SCDA Architects throughout my architectural journey. The creation of this monograph, the fourth in the architectural series and the 7th book in the overall SCDA collection, is a milestone documenting 11 years of work, starting from 2013 to 2024. It is timely as 2025 marks the 30th anniversary of SCDA Architects.

The book would not have been possible without the collective efforts and contributions of many dedicated clients, professionals, consultants, contractors, and colleagues.

First and foremost, I would like to extend my heartfelt gratitude to my family, whose unwavering support and encouragement have been a constant source of inspiration. My wife, Ling, has been my rock, offering unconditional love and understanding throughout the long hours and challenging moments.

To my directors and associates at SCDA Architects, I thank you for your trust, guidance, and collaboration. Your expertise, creativity, and camaraderie have been invaluable. To my staff and colleagues at SCDA Architects, I am proud of your dedication and spirit. Your tireless efforts, creativity, and commitment to excellence have made a significant impact on our projects and our firm's success. I am honored to work alongside such a talented and passionate team.

To our esteemed clients across many continents, I appreciate the faith you have placed in us, entrusting us with your vision and aspirations. Your confidence has driven us to push boundaries and strive for excellence.

I would also like to acknowledge the contributions of our consultants and contractors, whose specialized knowledge and skills have been instrumental in bringing our designs to life. Your professionalism and dedication have been exceptional, and I am grateful for your partnership.

The photographs in this book are a testament to the skill and artistic vision of photographers Aaron Pocock, Xiao Shi Hao, Amir Sultan, Finbarr Fallon, and others, who have captured the essence of our designs. Your ability to convey the beauty and formal compositions, capturing the spatial qualities of our buildings, has been invaluable.

The book designers Sonia Castillo and Victoria Lee have done an exceptional job in bringing this monograph to life. Your creativity, patience, and attention to detail have resulted in a visually stunning publication that I am proud to call my own. The written words and insights by Julia van den Hout and Leon van Schaik have provided valuable context and insights, offering a deeper understanding of our designs and philosophy. Your contributions have enriched this publication and are greatly appreciated.

Lastly, I would like to express my gratitude to Gordon Goff and the team at ORO Editions for their infinite patience and their belief in this project, and their dedication to producing a high-quality publication. Your professionalism and expertise have been instrumental in bringing this monograph to fruition.

Thank you all again for your unwavering support, guidance, and collaboration. This monograph is a testament to the power of passion, teamwork, dedication, and the pursuit of excellence.

Principal
Soo K Chan

Soo K Chan—AIA, FSIA, RIBA

Soo K Chan is a practicing architect based in Singapore and New York. He is the founding principal and design director of SCDA, a multi-disciplinary firm engaging in architecture, interior, landscape, lighting, and product design. A graduate from Yale University, Mr. Chan has lectured and taught at several international universities and is currently a professor of Architecture at the National University of Singapore (NUS).

SCDA's portfolio ranges from master planning, resorts and hotels, mixed-use developments and high-rise luxury residences, spanning Asia/Oceania, Africa, Europe, and America. In addition to architecture practice, Mr. Chan has been involved in designing, developing, and managing his own sustainable hospitality brand Soori, with completed projects in Bali, New York and Penang. Projects in Niseko and Wyoming are currently under development.

Through SCDA Lab and the Soori Fund, he has spearheaded social and cultural initiatives to advance the environmental cause.

Collaborators
SCDA 2013–24

Malcolm Fraser McCulloch—SIA

Malcolm McCulloch is a Director at SCDA with over 25 years of experience in architecture and landscape design, working globally throughout the U.S, Middle East and Asia. Graduating from the University of Strathclyde, UK in 1996, he received his professional registration with the Singapore Board of Architects in 2005.

Oon Jin Aik—ARB (UK), RIBA, SIA

Oon Jin Aik is a UK-trained and registered architect in Singapore and the UK. He graduated from University of Manchester and obtained his Postgraduate Diploma in Architecture at UCL, Bartlett School of Architecture. He has worked extensively on master planning, architecture and landscape design for over 30 years.

PRINCIPAL Soo K Chan

DIRECTORS Baet Yeok Hoon, Edward Lau, **Joshua Cheam**, Lee Kit Hung, **Malcolm McCulloch**, **Oon Jin Aik**, Yap Shee Leng

ASSOCIATE DIRECTORS **Adele Sim**, Amber Jan, Du Yu, Joana Couto, Joao Lavrador, Johnston Kor, **Kun Tran**, Mark Chenchin, **Nehemia Sasongko**, Ng Kok Yang, **Ong Lay Hinn**, **Sumina Surya**, **Winnie Ho**, Yeo Jia-Jun

SENIOR ASSOCIATES Alba Alonso, **Andrew Ng**, **Armand Devillard**, Chaveewan Chinalai, **Chin Wei Min**, Crystal Li, Edo Kartono, Faye Dy-Liacco, **Fu Yu**, Goh Lee Na, Hu Qi Wei, Jacqueline Judd, Lee Hyo Mi, **Leon Li**, **Lilian Dirgantoro**, **Marianne Ponce**, **Mark Beecroft**, Mauricio Gonzalez, **Qiu Jie**, **Tolis Apostolidis**, Wesley Liew

ASSOCIATES Aleksandra Koroleva, Amanda Tiong, Andrew Barrass, Angelica Noynay, Anna Petrungaro, **Audrey Wang**, Chen Cheng, **Chen Shuhua**, **Eric Wang**, Erickson Gopez, Feng Yao, **Feng Zitong**, Fion Li, **Guo Zhaoning**, Hwajung Song, **Janice Arrubio**, Jessica Baczkowski, **Joey Wong**, Jonathan Dolan, Joyce Heng, **Katrina Aliño-Maloom**, Koh Jin Yu, **Kuang Yuefan**, Leslie Xia, **Lim Chiuyee**, Lim Yin Shi, Lin Lijun, **Livina Rahmayanti**, **Lois Kok**, **Lorrie Besmonte**, Low Yan Horng, **Lu Na**, Makhasiri Khanoei, Maki Yukari, Mariana Charters, Mou Yuyangguang, Ong Wee Jin, Paulina Szczepaniak, Richard Mirasol, Ronilo Gabon, Ronnie Santos, Sharon Wong, Shirlyn Low, **Stanley Tan**, Ukrit Thongthammachat, **Wahyuni Kurniawati**

COLLABORATORS Aaron Soh, Adeline Lau, Agnes Tjipto, Agnieszka Omastka, Ahnanchana Srichamara, Aileen Cervantes, Alex Wong, Alexandra Whittenburg, Alwyn Soh, Amanda Chin, **Amanda Moore**, Anjamarie Gaztambide, Anna Kwon, Bahruddin Bin Hussein, Benjamin Lee, Bernie Ang, Bi Zhouxi, Bin Yeo, Brandon Chin, Carolina Cancerinadewi, Carrie Yan, Cattani Stella, Charles Liu, Chawalit Tharaumpawan, Chen Shufei, Chen Zexin, Cheng Rui Chween, Cheryl Pang, Chew Boyang, Chiang Sze May, Chloe Tan, **Cho Bong Jun**, Chong Shu Mun, Chong Wei Rong, Christian Galan, Christian Lam, **Christina Seow**, Christopher Esper, Chua Jia Yu, **Chua Minchi**, Chua Sheng Kang, **Claire Feng**, Csaba Babud, Dai Bing, **Damon Shi**, Echo Yang, Eileen Koh, Eilen Tan, **Ekkachai Pongyim**, **Eling Zhu**, **Elizabeth Lum**, Eng Sui Kee, **Er Chen Wei**, Eri Kanno, **Eric Balaan**, Eric Baldwin, Erika Koh, Erika Zhang, Esther Lau, Esther Oi, Eugene Lim, **Eunice Ling**, Fadlon Binti A Bakar, Felicia Lee, **Ferline Tan**, Fu Ting Ting, Fumiko Okuwaki, **Gabriel Kioshima**, Gabriel Quan, **Gao Min**, Gemma Lim, **Gianfranco Piguing**, Goh Guat Lay, Goh Shu Lan, Grace Ho, Gregory Barber, **Hakeem Hausely**, **Han Yun Chou**, **Han Huichao**, Harmony Wee, He Liao, Henry Ang, Ho Jun Kang, **Husaini Bin Zain**, **Ignatius Lee**, Imelda Villaflor, Iris Wang, Ivan Soh, Jacqueline Goh, Jacqueline Ong, Jade Hubinek, James Chidiac, **Janet Soo**, Janice Kwa, Jaryl Tng, **Jason Loria**, Jay-R Mendoza, Jeannette Foo, Jeong Youngjin, Jenny Lian, **Jesse Mendoza**, Jessica Yunnaraga, **Jessie Teo**, Ji Qi An, **John Chia**, John Li, John Vencer, John-Nathan Chan, Johnson Chng, Jon Ivan De Guzman, Jonathan Ng, Josefina Agumbay, Joshua Seow, **Joshuel Chan**, Jovian Legimun, Judy Wong, Kan Fook Seng, Kang Ho-Jun, Kang Yu Mee, Karren Ticzon, Katie Engelmeyer, **Kelly Tan**, **Kenny Choo**, Kevin He, Khiu Chwee Choon, **Kingsley Tan**, Koh Hau Yeow, Lam Poh Leong, **Lee Jin Ting**, **Lee Lip Jiang**, Leryn Wong, Lesley-Anne Maza, **Li Lang**, **Li Xin Lei**, Lim Jea Imm, Lim Wei Ling, Lim Yee Cheng, **Liu Boyu**, Liu Jin Rong, Liu Ping, Loke Foong Ming, **Lorraine Pang**, Louis Chua, Lu Wenwen, **Lu Zhichao**, Lucas Djunaedy, Luisiani Pawitan, Luke Guo, Luo Jing Wen, **Manthakorn Chailangka**, **Matthew Goh**, Marcella Lim, Marina Archangeli, Marina Milosavljevic, Mark Nepomuceno, Mark Vijaykumar, Mars Kueh, **Mary Jane Bermas**, Maulana Islami, Megan Berry, Michael Fabian, Michele Lau, Michele Leow, Mildred Gascon, Monika Shen, Montarat Kasemsuvan, Mylene Lopez, Myra Mabango, Natalie Kung, Nathalia Kasman, **Neo Sze Hui**, Nguyen Anh Vu, Nguyen Tien Dung, Nicholas Gumulya, **Nicole Ang**, Nursyahidah Binte Mazlan, Paper Yang, Peggy Lee, Phylicia Tan, Poh Chai Ling, Porsha Teo, Qi Yi, Rachel Reinhard, Rachel Zhang, Raeesa D/O Mohammad Ilyas, Rebecca Shen, Renato Bael Cruzado, **Rhyna Chen**, Ronnie Santos, Ruiqi Zhou, Samuel Soine, **Sandy Wang**, Sara Abd Rabbo, Sean Dula, Sean Liu, **Sem Jia Le**, **Serene Hue**, **Shawn Xiao**, **Sheridan Vinluan**, Sia Lee, Siriwan Thongprasert, Siti Nur Aisah Binte Juma'at, Stacy Chung, **Stan Yu**, Suzannah Grasel, Tan Kae Ming, Tan Si Hua, Tang Hoay Nee, Tang Yin Yi, Tanya Valderrama, **Tao Hu Vince**, Tay Aik Wen, Tay Sue Ismail, Taylor Halamka, Taylor Zhai Williams, Tey Shu Fen, Tobias Low, **Tommy Wang**, Tong Jinfang, **Troy Alcala**, **Victoria Lee**, Vivien Neoh, Vo Van Huong, Vorapol Laovoravinyoo, Wang Hui, Wang Ziwen, Warren Tey, Wendelyn Salas-Luzano, Wilsara Lloren, Wong Bih Fang, Wong Wing See, Wu Lin, Xaviera Wong, Xie Qilin, Xienny Lew, **Xu Qing**, Xuan Zeyi, **Yan Jiawei**, **Yang Fan**, Yap Xiao Yao, Yap Yee Chen, **Ye Ziwei**, Yeh Hong Yee, Yio Chee Kiang, Yuan Yijia, Yuhan Bian, **Yuhan Zhang**, Yvonne Chew, Zachary Ho, Zeng Zhibin, Zhang Wenting, Zheng Haotian, Zheng Junru, Zhou Mo, Zhu Ying Ling, Zoe Lin

Current staff are in bold (correct at the time of print)

ORO Editions
Publishers of Architecture, Art and Design
Gordon Goff: Publisher

www.oroeditions.com
info@oroeditions.com

Published by ORO Editions

Author: Soo Khian Chan
Foreword: Soo Khian Chan
Essay: Julia van den Hout
Leon van Schaik
Book Design: Sonia Castillo Studio
SCDA Architects
Managing Editor: Jake Anderson

10 9 8 7 6 5 4 3 2 1 First Edition

ISBN: 978-1-961856-55-4

Color Separations and Printing: ORO Group Inc.
Printed in China

ORO Editions makes a continuous effort to minimize the overall carbon footprint of its publications. As part of this goal, ORO Editions, in association with Global ReLeaf, arranges to plant trees to replace those used in the manufacturing of the paper produced for its books. Global ReLeaf is an international campaign run by American Forests, one of the world's oldest nonprofit conservation organizations. Global ReLeaf is American Forests' education and action program that helps individuals, organizations, agencies, and corporations improve the local and global environment by planting and caring for trees.

Image Credits
Aaron Pocock: 14–15, 22–23, 57–59, 63–67, 74, 80, 83–86, 88–89, 108–110, 112–119, 121–122, 132–136, 138–143, 145–149, 184, 186–191, 194–197, 198–201, 228, 230–233, 264, 266–272, 274–277, 286, 288–291, 293, 300, 302–309, 322, 324–326, 328–329, 364, 366–371, 378–379, 394, 397
Aey Srirath Somsawat: 82, 85
Arch-Exist: 6–7, 34, 227
Client (The Lalu Hotel): 192, 197, 201, 400–401
Client (Vanke OCT Nanchang): 358
Finbarr Fallon: 98, 100–107, 166, 168–176, 178–183, 254, 256–263, 282–283
Kadek: 332, 334–335
Lei Tan Tan: 34, 37, 159, 162–165
Lei Yun Yun: 30, 33, 35–36
Li Rui: 152–153, 318, 320–321
On Maja's Map: 330
Pure Pixel Photography: 226–227
Raquel Diniz: 77
Robert Kleiner: 393
SCDA: All other images
Seth Powers: 222, 224–225
Tim Williams: 60–62
UJIN: 202, 204–207, 209
Urban: 321
Vinay Panjwani: 234, 236–237
Xiao Shi Hao: 26, 30–31, 42, 44–53, 158–159, 162, 388–389
Zhang Zhao: 124–131
Zhu Hai: 154, 156–157